The Pharaoh Factor:

Living with a Hardened Heart

A DEVOTIONAL

KEVIN P. HORATH

LUCIDBOOKS

The Pharaoh Factor
Living with a Hardened Heart: A Devotional
Copyright © 2018 by Kevin P. Horath

Published by Lucid Books in Houston, TX
www.LucidBooksPublishing.com

All Scripture quotations are taken from the King James Version (KJV): King James Version, public domain.

ISBN-10: 1-63296-242-X
ISBN-13: 978-1-63296-242-3
eISBN-10: 1-63296-243-8
eISBN-13: 978-1-63296-243-0

Special Sales: Most Lucid Books titles are available in special quantity discounts. Custom imprinting or excerpting can also be done to fit special needs. Contact Lucid Books at Info@LucidBooksPublishing.com.

For Joe Stricklin
He lived his life with a "Blazing Call"

Table of Contents

Preface

Aheavy heart is different than a hardened heart. Much different. As you read this book, I trust you will learn what it means to live with a hardened heart and how to effectively treat this common spiritual condition. However, as I write this preface on March 30, 2018, my heart is heavy. You see, today I had to say my earthly farewell to a mentor and friend—Joe Stricklin.

My name is Kevin Horath, associate pastor at Hillside Bethel Tabernacle in Decatur, Illinois. This is the second book I have written in what I hope to be a series, and I have discovered it is a never-ending process. While a chapter may end, a book may end, and even an individual life may end, life continues on. Pages are still being written. There is always a story to tell.

God has blessed me and my family over the years. My father, Pastor Donald E. Horath, founded Hillside in 1961 and has been its pastor ever since. Through the ministry of Hillside, I have been introduced to many pastors, evangelists, apostles, teachers, and prophets. Many have gone on to be with the Lord. Some are still in ministry today. And all these men and women have had an eternal impact on my life and on the lives many others.

But Joe, in particular, was perhaps the strongest influence in my life. He was an evangelist I met in the early 1980s when he came to our church. He returned numerous times over the years to minister to our local congregation. He went to our youth camps. He stayed in our home. I was blessed to get to know him personally, and I learned a lot from him. When I was a teenager, he was the role model I desperately needed.

As commonly happens to all of us in our relationships in some form or another, our roads eventually diverged, and life took us on different paths. We lost contact for a while. However, when we reconnected, it was as though no time had passed. We picked up right where we left off and helped each other through various phases of our lives.

About six weeks ago, feeling tired physically and spiritually, I asked Joe if he remembered a short story he had written and shared with me several years ago. It was a word of encouragement, and I couldn't find it. Neither could he. He searched. I searched. It was almost like it was not meant to be found. We let it go, and then on March 20, 2018, I sent him the first draft of this book to review for me. He let me know that he received it and that he would be honored to review it. On Monday, March 26, 2018, at 6:30 p.m., I learned that Joe had unexpectedly passed away. Unfortunately, I don't know whether he had the chance to review the manuscript. We did not have the opportunity to speak again. It seems as though there were several things left undone that we would never get to finalize in this life. That saddens me.

Because of my grief, I went back and reviewed the many emails from Joe that I had exchanged. I wanted to reminisce a little. This time, I found the short story Joe had written. While it does not directly deal with a hardened heart or this book in particular, it is still relevant. It was meant to be found. It just had to be found at the right time, which makes the words even more meaningful and precious. So to honor my friend, I will share his email and vision right here before we begin this study of Pharaoh. This is what Joe said to me in 2014:

~~~~~~~~~~~~~~~~~~~~~~~~~~~~~~~~~~~~

I believe the Lord has "saved the best wine for the last," for me and you both, Kevin. The best may be yet to come. So I say, "Bring on those new wine skins and pour it in. And then, pour me out again!"

I can't put my finger on it (just yet), bro, but something's stirring. There's a shaking coming, and it has even already begun. God is raising up something. He's given me a vision of a soldier come back from battle. He hangs his gunpowder-stained musket over the fireplace as an emblem of days now over. As he sits back in his easy chair, he lights his pipe and gazes into the fire, remembering the terrible battles, the fearfulness of it all. He remembers fellow soldiers, his band of brothers, praying, going hungry, surviving, and dying together. He closes his eyes in relief as he realizes he's finally home safe. It's all over.

The soldier can't think of much he misses about war. But still, something seems hollow in him. What is it? Surely, there's nothing about those fighting days he would dare ever want to go back to. After all, his bones have become so tired now. That time he was wounded still hurts when the cold rains come. And that fire feels so good.

Then, as he sits in the silence, the popping fire about to whisper him into a nice long sleep, there comes a distant rumbling. Could it be? Surely not! But yes, it is! He hears another. And suddenly, it's his brothers! They're shouting, "Get your gun, soldier! The enemy's a-comin' over the hill! Let's go get 'em! Let's send them dirty [blanks] to hell where they belong!"

As the old warrior reaches up over the fireplace to grab his gun, fear rushes back. The old leg wound makes him cringe as he jumps up out of his easy chair. The cold rain hits him in the face as he storms into the night. And as he runs up the hill to face the enemy, an all too familiar feeling comes over him.

Suddenly, for just an instant, he remembers what it was that must have made him feel so hollow and empty just seconds before.

It was the fire he once felt in his belly! The thing that made him know he was alive! And now, it's back!

The Lord would say, "Can you hear it? It's time to go grab your gun, boys!"

Hahaha!

I love you, brother, Kevin Horath.

I'll see ya soon,

Joe

~~~~~~~~~~~~~~~~~~~~~~~~

Joe's signature song that he wrote and sang was "Blazing Call." It was the way he lived his life—not perfect yet always wanting to be used for Christ. He had a heart for God, and so he also had a heart for people. He wanted to always be in the battle. That battle was not *against* people, it was *for* people. I am proud to be counted as one among the thousands that he influenced for Christ in that spiritual battle.

Now Joe is gone. He ran his race. He finished his course. He kept his faith. What seems in the natural too soon, God has in perfect control. We just cannot allow our hearts to be hardened to what God is doing. That is the major lesson of this book. It has also been a major lesson in my life.

So, to Joe I say, *thank you for the lessons you have taught me, even in your death. I hope you were able to read the words of this book before you passed. I would have loved to have heard your thoughts. Even so, I love you, too, brother. Indeed, we will see each other soon.*

For the rest of us, thank you for joining me and reading this book. Let's begin this study and apply its lessons.

May we, like Joe, live our lives with a blazing call.

Introduction

Who was the Pharaoh of the Exodus? The Exodus account in the Old Testament does not mention him by his proper name, just by his title. Since Moses was the author of the book of Exodus, he certainly should have known Pharaoh's name since he had direct dealings with him. Moses may have even grown up with him in the palace. But Moses did not use his name in his writings.

Why not?

It is quite possible that Moses did not call him by name for a specific reason. In Exodus 5:2, Moses records Pharaoh as asking, "Who is the LORD that I should obey his voice to let Israel go?" Here, Pharaoh calls God by his name. That is evidenced by the word LORD, which is used in place of the proper name of God throughout scripture. However, Pharaoh did not know Yahweh personally.

The irony here is that while we do not know Pharaoh's name, we do know the Lord's name—Yahweh. So it seems that part of Moses's intent in writing the book of Exodus was not to exalt the Egyptian Pharaoh, who was considered to be a divine god-king, but rather to glorify the one true God of Israel—by name. That is speculation, but it is a possibility.

Nevertheless, while the goal is not to exalt Pharaoh of the Exodus, there is still a lot we can learn from him. When conducting a character study, we often choose heroes we can model. We did that in *The Elisha Factor* by studying the Old Testament prophet Elisha. It is also sometimes helpful to study characters that display behaviors we should not emulate. Even though we often learn the hard way—through our own experiences—maybe we can learn from the mistakes of others and recognize the same dangers within ourselves before they actually happen to us.

This book is one such study.

Pharaohs in the Bible

The Bible makes reference to various pharaohs of Egypt. They include unnamed pharaohs in Genesis and Exodus as well as a number of named rulers in other books. When they are named, it helps scholars place approximate dates and times on biblical events because they correspond with other historical documents.

For example, 2 Kings 19:9 refers to Tirhakah, the king of Ethiopia. Isaiah 37:9 refers to the same king. And 2 Kings 23:29 and 2 Chronicles 35:20 mention Nechoh, a pharaoh and a king who was responsible for the death of Josiah. Jeremiah 44:30 mentions Hophra, the pharaoh who succeeded Nechoh. The naming of these rulers helps identify the chronology of events from a world history perspective.

But the pharaohs mentioned in the books of Genesis and Exodus are unidentified by name. Historians and scholars have attempted to name them to help place the events on the timeline of world history. Movies such as *The Ten Commandments* and *The Prince of Egypt* have gone so far as to name some of them. Are they correct? We do not know for sure. Moses chose not to identify those leaders, and we are left to make educated guesses.

Since we do not know their names, it is important to look at their stories. They are mentioned in scripture, although often just as supporting characters or antagonists. However, they are there for a reason. The first pharaoh is recorded in Genesis 12:10–20 as Abram journeyed to Egypt in order to escape a famine in Canaan. Pharaoh heard about the beauty of Sarai, Abram's wife, and she was summoned to meet him. Because of her, Abram gained favor with the Pharaoh and acquired livestock and servants. However, Abram did not exactly tell the truth about his relationship with Sarai. Pharaoh wanted to make Sarai his wife, but God in response sent plagues upon Pharaoh. When this happened, Pharaoh discovered Sarai's true relationship with Abram and released her. Then he ordered Abram to take his goods and get out of Egypt.

The next pharaoh is mentioned in the last chapters of the book of Genesis in the story of Joseph. In Genesis 37–50, Joseph, the son of Israel (formerly Jacob), was sold by his brothers into Egyptian slavery. God blessed Joseph, and he was promoted by the unnamed Pharaoh to be the vizier of Egypt. During a subsequent famine, Joseph was given permission to bring his father, his brothers, and all their family to live in Egypt. While that was a great story of salvation, these events set up the conditions for the story of another pharaoh nearly 400 years later, recorded in Exodus.

The Israelites were no longer welcome guests in Egypt as they were during the time of Joseph. They overstayed their welcome and became enslaved. When we look at the story in Exodus, we see that there were actually two pharaohs involved in the story. At the beginning of Exodus is the Pharaoh of the Oppression, who died while Moses was in exile. He was succeeded by the Pharaoh of the Exodus, during whose rule the Israelites escape.

It is the Pharaoh of the Exodus that we will study.

The Humanity of the Pharaoh of the Exodus

Many stories and movies today often portray the main villain simply as a flawed human being. Sometimes, the antagonist is not so much evil as he or she is misunderstood. Or perhaps the situations in these stories cause the villains to act or react in a way they would otherwise not behave. In other words, it makes the villain more relatable—more like us—and more human.

I remember this type of character development in the movie *Spider-Man 3*. One character, Sandman, was a man who entered a life of crime in order to get healthcare for his daughter. It was not that he was a bad person. He just found himself in a difficult situation. He did what he had to do in order to help his daughter. What father wouldn't do the same? Hollywood did something similar to the villain called Vulture in the newer *Spider-Man: Homecoming* movie. They made the character human, a man trying to provide for his family.

That concept frustrated me at first. I found it frustrating because it implies that people are not really bad or all that evil—they just find themselves in bad situations. When we see it that way, it can be unnerving because we discover that we, but for the grace of God, could find ourselves in a similar situation. That brings it too close to home. I want a clear line between good and evil people, and I want to be on the side of good. If the line is not clear, then how would I act in that type of situation? Could I cross that line? Are all bad guys human with some good left in them, like Darth Vader in *Star Wars*? Or is there really pure evil in the world that is beyond redemption?

We know that we are all born in sin and formed in iniquity. The Bible tells us that. It means none of us are good on our own. Evil lurks within us all, waiting to manifest itself. Yet we must be careful to not give evil a human face. The apostle Paul instructs us not to battle against flesh and blood because our battle is a spiritual one. Therefore, we must realize that villains, even our enemies, are still human and, therefore, loved by God. And then it hit me. Jesus died for even the vilest of sinners. These movies make a valid point about the humanity of the villains. Wow!

While villains can be portrayed as human in the movies, they are more so in real life. Therefore, we must not be happy when our real-life villains find themselves in trouble (Prov. 24:17) or find pleasure when they die (Ezek. 18:23). Rather, we must love our enemies (Matt.

5:44). We must pray for them. This point was driven home for me when I heard the news about the death of Osama bin Laden. Truly, if anyone deserved to die, it was him, right? Many people celebrated his death. They rejoiced that this evil man was eliminated from Earth. It was a great day for justice.

I found myself, however, unable to rejoice in his death. Of course, I was thankful for justice. I was glad he was found and stopped. Even though I remembered the death, destruction, and heartache he had caused, I just could not celebrate the fact that he died. As I reflected on the news, I remembered that Jesus died for Osama bin Laden, too. Jesus loved him. Osama's choices and his death, no doubt, broke God's heart. All of it did. Yet, governments and officials are ordained by God to handle this very thing. Justice had to be done.

This may seem like a contradiction, but it is not. I accepted the justice that was administered, and I agreed with it. I still do. On a personal level, though, I could not bring myself to celebrate his death. I just could not be happy that he died, even as necessary as it was. The villain was human, and his death did not eliminate evil from the world. It never does.

Only one death (and resurrection) eliminates evil. Therefore, we must do as Jesus commanded. Love our enemies. Pray for our enemies. Even bless our enemies. Allow the authorities and God to take care of vengeance and justice. It is hard, but that is not all we must do. We can also learn from our enemies. It is important that we avoid falling into the same mistakes and sins. Perhaps their lives can serve as a warning to us all. The book of Proverbs gives us wise advice and warnings about these types of matters. Pharaoh's life is one such warning, too. But at the end of it all, he was still a human being loved by God. And he struggled. We should never forget that.

While Exodus gives us a picture of redemption through the story of the Passover, it is also a lesson about what happens when we rebel against God. Up to that point in history, God was not known by his proper name—Yahweh—but only as God almighty. Now we know his name. Pharaoh did, too, and chose to go toe-to-toe with the God of the Hebrews. Maybe that is why Moses did not name him. Maybe Moses did not want to give Pharaoh any glory for taking God head on. If so, we will not exalt him, either. Yet, there is still much to learn from him. And so we will.

In this study, we will investigate some of the characteristics or factors of the humanity of Pharaoh of the Exodus. Since he was in opposition to God, we will use some phrases that, as acronyms, spell GOD backwards.

Factor One:	Privileged	Descendant of Greatness
Factor Two:	Ignorant	Delusions of Grandeur
Factor Three:	Unbelieving	Doubts of God
Factor Four:	Disobedient	Deformity of Godliness
Factor Five:	Uncaring	Devoid of Guilt
Factor Six:	Foolish	Decisions of Greed
Factor Seven:	Hardened	Disposition of Granite
Factor Eight:	Lost	Destiny or Grace

Who knows? We may even learn some other things along the way—things about Pharaoh and things about ourselves. So hang on as we dive into the study—The Pharaoh Factor.

Factor One:
Descendant of Greatness

*But as many as received him, to them gave he power
to become the sons of God, even to them that believe
on his name: Which were born, not of blood, nor of
the will of the flesh, nor of the will of man, but of God.*
—John 1:12–13

Throughout history, many leaders have come into power because of their lineage. In genealogy, royal descent is sometimes claimed as a mark of distinction and seen as a desirable attribute. Having descended from a past or present monarch can provide many benefits, including fame, fortune, power, and all the great things that come with such an esteemed status.

That has happened in many nations and kingdoms. Even though monarchies may not actually rule any longer in some nations, their influence can still be great. Consider the royal family in the United Kingdom. Although the monarch no longer has a political or executive role in government, she continues to play an important part in the life of the nation. Queen Elizabeth acts as a symbol of national identity, unity, and pride. She gives a sense of stability, continuity, and tradition. And in all monarchies, the king or queen is supported by members of his or her immediate family. Indeed, the royal bloodline is important and, in their countries, must be nurtured and preserved.

Similarly, the most powerful person in ancient Egypt was none other than the pharaoh. Deemed the political and religious leader of the Egyptian people, the pharaoh owned all the land, made the laws, collected taxes, and commissioned armies to defend the nation from foreigners. Also, the pharaoh, according to the country's religious belief system, represented the gods on Earth. As such, he performed rituals and built cities and temples to honor the gods.

Because of this great responsibility, ancient Egyptian royal families were almost always expected to marry within the family. They did that because they believed it was necessary to keep their bloodline completely pure. Historians believe inbreeding happened in just about every Egyptian dynasty. In some cases, the result of inbreeding led to defects, disorders, and even stillbirths. Taken too far, a pharaoh would eventually not produce a successor and would become the last of his dynasty. In a paradoxical twist of fate, the very thing that was supposed to preserve the dynasty ultimately led to its ruin.

That is most likely what happened to Tutankhamun, commonly known as King Tut. He was the last of his dynasty because all his children were stillborn. The line ended with him. That happened time and again in various dynasties and with a variety of rulers. This factor of being a descendant of greatness may have also played into the character of the Pharaoh of the Exodus. Who knows? At the very least, he was no doubt influenced and pressured by the successes of his ancestors. The weight and responsibility of ruling effectively had to be great. His father, the Pharaoh of the Oppression, was successful in enslaving the Hebrews. Under his rule, great cities were built.

Therefore they did set over them taskmasters to afflict them with their burdens. And they built for Pharaoh treasure cities, Pithom and Raamses.

—Exod. 1:11

However, as will happen to all of us, the Pharaoh of the Oppression eventually died. A new Pharaoh assumed power and, in the natural, he was a descendant of greatness. How would he carry on the family name? What would he do of great national importance? What would he accomplish to add his name to the long line of successes achieved by his family? How would he be remembered in the annuls of history?

But [God] overthrew Pharaoh and his host in the Red sea: for his mercy endureth for ever.

—Ps. 136:15

According to the Bible, he would not do so great.

Genealogy in the Bible

Perhaps part of Pharaoh's problem was that he had a royal bloodline. It is possible that many of the decisions he made came from the pressure of upholding the family name. Maybe he thought he was really something because of his family heritage. That is not uncommon today, either.

However, it is not our genealogy that is the problem. The Bible contains multiple genealogical records. They are an important part of scripture. Used appropriately, our own genealogy can be influential in our lives. But for a moment, consider why biblical genealogies are helpful.

First, they help substantiate the Bible's historical accuracy. While the Bible is a book of faith, it is also a book of history. The genealogies, while not necessarily fun to read, confirm the existence of characters in the Bible. In fact, these characters were more than just characters.

They were actual, living, breathing, humans. The Bible is truth. And it is also historic truth. Genealogies help us confirm that.

Biblical genealogies also help us see the fulfillment of prophecy. For instance, it was prophesied that the Messiah would come through the line of Jesse, through his son David. Isaiah 11:1 says, "And there shall come forth a rod out of the stem of Jesse, and a Branch shall grow out of his roots."

God confirmed who Jesus is by recording his lineage in scripture. We find his genealogy in Matthew 1:1–17 and Luke 3:23–38. Yes, the genealogy of Jesus is one proof, among many, of Jesus's fulfillment of Old Testament prophecies.

And finally, genealogies are just practical. They give us glimpses into the lives of the people in the Bible. Even in the most detailed of stories, we only receive a glimpse of what happened day in and day out. Yet in those glimpses, we see God working in both big and small ways. We see God working through the lives of Jewish people. We also see God working in the lives of the Gentiles. Did you know that Ruth and Rahab were both Gentiles in the Messianic line? It is true.

That is because God values people. He values individuals. While he uses our families and our circumstances, it is not about that. He does not really care about your pedigree. He cares about having a personal relationship with you—no matter where you come from. He just cares about where you are going. Galatians 3:26–29 makes this clear:

> For ye are all the children of God by faith in Christ Jesus. For as many of you as have been baptized into Christ have put on Christ. There is neither Jew nor Greek, there is neither bond nor free, there is neither male nor female: for ye are all one in Christ Jesus. And if ye be Christ's, then are ye Abraham's seed, and heirs according to the promise.

In *The Elisha Factor: Living the Double-Portion Life*, there is a parallel principle. It is not our natural bloodline that is important. The only blood that really matters belongs to Jesus. When we trust him, we are adopted children of God. We are heirs of God. But more than that, we are joint heirs with Jesus. We are entitled to a double-portion inheritance.

Practical Application

Unfortunately, we often put too much emphasis on our natural heritage. If we are not careful, we can allow favoritism, nepotism, and natural qualifications to interfere with the supernatural functioning of the body of Christ. When we put faith in our pedigree, it puts us at odds with God (and God's people). That is just what happened with Pharaoh.

The Old Testament demonstrates how physical leadership in Egypt and other monarchies was passed along to physical descendants. However, the New Testament advocates no such practice. In fact, the appointment of church leaders was to be done without favoritism of any kind. In 1 Timothy 5:21 we read, "I charge thee before God, and the Lord Jesus Christ, and the elect angels, that thou observe these things without preferring one before another, doing nothing by partiality."

The Holy Spirit enables and empowers leaders to serve effectively and sovereignly gives them these gifts. The church recognizes these gifts and then places individuals into ministry situations. But the anointing must come before the appointing.

> *Wherefore, brethren, look ye out among you seven men of honest report, full of the Holy Ghost and wisdom, whom we may appoint over this business.*
> —Acts 6:3

Granting leadership positions to family members (or others), regardless of the anointing, is not a New Testament method of appointing leaders or church staff. Does that mean that family members are disqualified from serving or being appointed to leadership positions? Of course not! Neither are family members automatically qualified just because they are in a certain family. That can be a touchy subject in a church and one that, quite frankly, is very common. I know about it all too well. Let me explain.

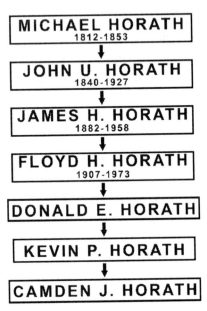

I recently discovered something about my family tree. This flow chart shows the direct Horath family line that goes through me. There are, of course, many, many other branches, and this is just one line that thankfully is still growing. If you ever study your own genealogy, you will probably find it quite exciting, humbling, and, in some ways, surreal.

I do not know a lot about my ancestors. I do know that Michael Horath lived in Germany and died there at the age of 41. His son John moved to America and settled in Effingham County, Illinois. Why there? I do not know. But my family lived there until my grandfather, Floyd (Highpockets) Horath, moved to Decatur, Illinois. I have fleeting memories of my grandfather. I was only three years old when he passed away. They are all good memories—very good.

That is mainly all I know about my direct natural lineage. Most of my memories, which are still being made, involve my father, Donald E. Horath, and now my son, Camden J. Horath. These men have been and always will be among the most important men in my life. And to make things even better, my father is also my pastor. And that is where there have been some issues.

Because of our natural relationship, there have been accusations over the years regarding God's call on my life. Many years ago, I received a vicious anonymous letter about my life, my position, my parents, and the so-called Church of Horath. That letter hurt me immensely, especially since I was going through one of the most difficult times of my life, up to that point anyway. Because of that letter, other accusations, and some life events, I stopped and examined my life, my motives, and my call. In some ways, that was a good thing, because I wanted to make sure I was anointed and not just appointed. It had to be God. I had to be sure.

And, yes, I am sure.

To be transparent, there have been times when I placed family first—maybe too much sometimes. I am, unapologetically, pro-family. I believe that is biblical. However, like Pharaoh, we can take it too far. We can rely on being a descendant of greatness. Yet as I examined my life, I found that I have sometimes gone to the extreme in the other direction. Not that I was anti-family, but I wanted to be successful on my own and not because of my family. The only way to do that was outside the church. Inside the church, my position was viewed as nepotism. So I tried to serve the local church without taking anything financial from it.

The apostle Paul knew full well that he had the right as an apostle to be supported financially by those to whom he was ministering. Nevertheless, he chose to waive that right, preaching the gospel at no cost, so the gospel would not be hindered. He did not want to be a burden to the churches he served by requiring them to support him. Acts 20:33–35 records Paul as saying:

> *I have coveted no man's silver, or gold, or apparel. Yea,*
> *ye yourselves know, that these hands have ministered*
> *unto my necessities, and to them that were with me.*
> *I have shewed you all things, how that so labouring*

ye ought to support the weak, and to remember the words of the Lord Jesus, how he said, It is more blessed to give than to receive.

Paul did this because of the anointing. It was not required, but it was best for the situation. Likewise, we must do what we do because of the anointing. Then, because of the anointing, we also accept the appointing. We recognize that others may not accept that and may not support our work in the ministry. And there may be challenges. Some may even come against us. I understand that. I get it. Yet we will not give up. We will not give in. We will not quit.

Why? Because it is not *an* anointing. It is *the* anointing. It comes from the Holy Ghost.

Therefore, we boast. But we do not boast in our flesh. We do not boast in our pedigree. We do not boast in what we want. We do not boast in what our family wants. We boast in the Lord and what he has done. Him. Alone.

In the LORD shall all the seed of Israel be justified, and shall glory.

—Isa. 45:25

Finally, my brethren, rejoice in the LORD. To write the same things to you, to me indeed is not grievous, but for you it is safe. Beware of dogs, beware of evil workers, beware of the concision. For we are the circumcision, which worship God in the spirit, and rejoice in Christ Jesus, and have no confidence in the flesh. Though I might also have confidence in the flesh. If any other man thinketh that he hath whereof he might trust in the flesh, I more: Circumcised the eighth day, of the stock of Israel, of the tribe of Benjamin, an Hebrew of the Hebrews; as touching the law, a Pharisee; Concerning zeal, persecuting the church; touching the righteousness which is in the law, blameless. But what things were gain to me, those I counted loss for Christ. Yea doubtless, and I count all things but loss for the excellency of the knowledge of Christ Jesus my LORD: for whom I have suffered the loss of all things, and do count them but dung, that I may win Christ, And be found in him, not having mine own righteousness, which is of the law, but that which is through faith of Christ, the righteousness which is of God by faith: That I may know him, and the power of his resurrection, and the fellowship of his sufferings, being made conformable unto his death; If by any means I might attain unto the resurrection of the dead. Not as though I had already attained, either were already perfect: but I follow after, if that I may apprehend that for which also I am apprehended of Christ Jesus.

—Phil. 3:1–12

Therein lies our confidence. It is not because we are a descendant of greatness. It is in the Lord. It is a lesson Pharaoh would have done well to learn.

The same is true for us.

Factors to Consider

1. How has your family tree (your genealogy) affected your life?

2. What are some positive traits or characteristics common to those in your family?

3. The Holy Spirit enables and empowers those in the church. How has the Holy Spirit empowered you?

4. How is the anointing of the Holy Spirit confirmed in your church?

5. What does it mean to boast in the Lord?

Factor Two:
Delusions of Grandeur

For I say, through the grace given unto me, to every
man that is among you, not to think of himself more
highly than he ought to think; but to think soberly,
according as God hath dealt to every man the measure
of faith.

—Rom. 12:3

Pharaoh had an addiction.

It was not a physical addiction. Something within his personality caused him to repeatedly act upon his instincts. His nature, his built-in drive caused him to rebel against God, keep the Hebrews in slavery, and even make their working conditions worse. What was his addiction? Himself. Somewhere in his psyche he needed the affirmation that he was in control. When challenged or threatened, he responded in fury. And that gave him a false sense of domination. He would do anything to prove he was Pharaoh—the god-king—even at the expense of losing everything.

Pharaoh also had a measure of faith. We all do. The problem was that Pharaoh placed his faith in the wrong things. He trusted in his army. He trusted in his magicians and his servants. He trusted in his pedigree. But ultimately and fatally, he trusted in himself. He was a legend in his own mind, and he had to prove it. That was his undoing.

As a result, God had to completely unravel the Egyptian's nerves with devastating plagues. There were 10 of them recorded in Exodus, and those plagues struck at the very heart of Egyptian society by impacting what their own nature gods were supposed to control. Water turned to blood. Hordes of frogs, locusts, and lice made life absolutely miserable. Boils caused physical pain. All light was darkened. With each of the plagues, God made his point very clearly. He was God, and Pharaoh was to let his people go.

But even after the death of the firstborn in all of Egypt, Pharaoh made one final mistake. He would not give up. He led his army straight into a watery grave.

Why did he do that?

It really does not make sense. To the logical observer, it had to have been clear that this contest with God was over. What person in his right mind, after seeing all the wonders God showed, would actually follow the Hebrews who were walking on dry land in the middle of a large body of water? After all the things Pharaoh just experienced, how could he not foresee that this decision was going to end badly? Even his servants, after the eighth plague, could see it was a lost cause.

> *And Pharaoh's servants said unto him, How long shall this man be a snare unto us? let the men go, that they may serve the LORD their God: knowest thou not yet that Egypt is destroyed?*
> —Exod. 10:7

His servants got it. Pharaoh did not. Deep down, he probably did know. However, his delusions of grandeur blinded him. He lost everything because he could not fight his own human nature. This is the ultimate warning to humankind: die to self, or it will be your ruin.

It is true whether you are running an empire, a country, a company, a church, or simply your own life.

Pharaoh's Relationship Delusions

Because of his delusions of grandeur, the Pharaoh of the Exodus refused to have a new and different relationship with the Hebrews. Times had changed. When the Hebrews first came to Egypt, they were welcomed by the Pharaoh who knew Joseph. They were guests in the land, and it was a great relationship. However, the next recorded pharaoh, the Pharaoh of the Oppression, did not know Joseph since more than 400 years had passed (Exod. 12:40, Acts 7:6, Gal. 3:17). In that time, the relationship between the two groups had changed for the worse. The Pharaoh of the Oppression said:

> *Come on, let us deal wisely with them; lest they multiply, and it come to pass, that, when there falleth out any war, they join also unto our enemies, and fight against us, and so get them up out of the land.*
>
> —Exod. 1:10

The Hebrews had become the Egyptians' slaves, but the Hebrews still prospered. The Pharaoh of the Oppression instituted methods of population control to try to keep them under control. As one would imagine, relationships between the Egyptians and the Hebrews were bad. However, the Pharaoh of the Exodus, when he came into power, had an opportunity to improve those relationships. The mistakes of his father did not have to define him. He could have been a different type of king. He could have made a positive difference. Unfortunately, that was not an option his ego would allow him to seriously consider. He totally disregarded Moses and Aaron when they asked for permission to sacrifice unto the Lord for just three days.

> *And the king of Egypt said unto them, Wherefore do*
> *ye, Moses and Aaron, let the people from their works?*
> *get you unto your burdens.*
> —Exod. 5:4

In other words, he said something like this: *Absolutely not! And by the way, just who do you think you are to allow the people to take a break from their work?* Not only did he refuse their request, he made their work even harder, refusing to give them straw to make bricks. The Hebrews now had to find their own straw and still make bricks at the same pace as when straw was provided. The Hebrews pleaded with Pharaoh, but to no avail. The divide between the Egyptians and the Hebrews grew.

> *And they said unto them, The Lord look upon you,*
> *and judge; because ye have made our savour to be*
> *abhorred in the eyes of Pharaoh, and in the eyes of his*
> *servants, to put a sword in their hand to slay us.*
> —Exod. 5:21

Pharaoh obviously felt threatened by any potential positive change in the relationship between the Egyptians and the Hebrews. And so, true to his nature, he responded in a way to preserve his power. He responded in anger. He responded in an extreme, negative manner far beyond what the situation required. Why? Simple. Because he could. He was Pharaoh. Any chance to bring peace and a positive relationship between the Egyptians and the Hebrews quickly spiraled out of control.

And it was all because Pharaoh thought too highly of himself. His power went to his head. He had delusions of grandeur, and it negatively impacted all his relationships.

Practical Application

What do you want most out of life? Many of us would rank healthy relationships—family, friends, coworkers, and on and on—high on that list. Relationships are at the center of our human existence. Everything we do involves people. Have you stopped to think about the relationship opportunities in your life? Is it possible that you are refusing to change old relationships that need repair or that you are closed to new relationships that God is bringing your way?

With the exception of knowing Jesus, healthy relationships make life enjoyable, perhaps more than anything else. Even if your health is not the best, if you have loving relationships, you can enjoy life. You can make millions of dollars and have a powerful sphere of influence, but if your relationships are broken or shallow, your life will be empty. A poor man with a loving family and good friends is far richer than a rich man who is poor relationally. We all probably know people who struggle with relationships. However, the question we really need to ask is this: Am I a person like that?

To be sure, a loving relationship with God is of first importance. Pharaoh had obviously failed in that respect (we'll explore that later). But loving relationships with others is of second importance. The Bible is all about these two important relationships—God and others.

> Jesus said unto him, Thou shalt love the LORD thy God with all thy heart, and with all thy soul, and with all thy mind. This is the first and great commandment. And the second is like unto it, Thou shalt love thy neighbour as thyself. On these two commandments hang all the law and the prophets.
>
> —Matt. 22:37–40

Because the Bible emphasizes healthy relationships so much, it is sad that there are so many of us who have hurting or broken relationships. Unlike Pharaoh, we know God. We have a personal relationship with Jesus. Yet many homes are still a dangerous battleground instead of a safe refuge. Even many Christian parents are at odds with their kids and, of course, the kids with their parents.

On the church level, some move from church to church, leaving a trail of destruction and damaged relationships in their wake. Some Christians will not even speak to other Christians because of misunderstandings, hurt feelings, and wrongs that have taken place both recently and in the far past.

These are just the tip of the iceberg when it comes to our relationship issues. We have all experienced damaged relationships in some form or another. Sadly, the loving families, genuine friendships, and healthy relationships we want most out of life sometimes mysteriously elude us.

But it should not be a mystery. In Romans 12, Paul gives the prescription for healthy relationships. Consistently practicing these qualities will produce healthy relationships. Unfortunately, that does not always happen. Relationships between two people take just that—two people. Both parties must be in active pursuit of a healthy relationship. Paul acknowledged that when he wrote this in Romans 12:18: "If it be possible, as much as lieth in you, live peaceably with all men."

The struggle is real. Isn't that the truth? Sometimes, no matter what you do, it is hard to get along with some people. But if you treat a difficult person with the qualities Paul speaks about, that relationship should, at the minimum, not get any worse. Do your part. In so doing, your relationships should get better. But even if some relationships never improve, if you relate to others as Paul describes in Romans 12, most of your relationships will be healthy.

Sure, that is easy to say, but it is not an easy instruction to apply. It is hard to implement. In order to develop these qualities, we must do what Pharaoh was unable or unwilling to do. We must examine ourselves. We must fully submit to God. We have to kill all immorality, impurity, passion, evil desire, and greed within us.

> *Mortify therefore your members which are upon the earth; fornication, uncleanness, inordinate affection, evil concupiscence, and covetousness, which is idolatry.*
>
> —Col. 3:5

In order to have healthy relationships, we have to put aside all anger, wrath, malice, slander, abusive speech, and lying (Col. 3:8–9). However, putting these things aside is not enough. We cannot just say no. We also have to say yes by putting on "bowels of mercies, kindness, humbleness of mind, meekness, longsuffering; Forbearing one another, and forgiving one another" (Col. 3:12–13).

The reason we must do this—the reason we *can* do this—is because God has graciously chosen and loved us. God's gracious, loving treatment of us is the basis for our treatment of others. In order to have healthy relationships, we must die to self. Pharaoh did not. He was addicted to self and therefore thought of himself more highly than he should have.

Now, do not go too far in the other direction. This does not mean we should think poorly of ourselves. No, just the opposite. We know who we are in Christ. Our righteousness in Christ will bring peace—peace of God, peace with God, peace with men, and peace with ourselves.

> *And the work of righteousness shall be peace; and the effect of righteousness quietness and assurance for ever.*
>
> —Isa. 32:17

Our self-esteem comes from who we are in Christ, not from our selfish delusions of grandeur and certainly not from what we try to prove before people. That type of pride will lead to one thing—a bitter end. Proverbs 16:18 says, "Pride goeth before destruction, and an haughty spirit before a fall."

Pharaoh assumed he was strong enough to win any battle. Is your pride making you think you are strong enough to fight even against God? Pharaoh thought the victories he had won in the past guaranteed all his victories. Are you relying on the past? Has your pride deluded you? Pharaoh never truly admitted he was wrong. In spite of contrary evidence and in spite of all that happened, he never really repented. He never admitted his mistakes. Is that how we are? If so, we are just like Pharaoh. We are full of delusions of grandeur. Pride-filled delusions will be our downfall.

The Pharaoh of the Exodus fell pretty hard. It did not have to happen that way. Sadly, he had total hatred for his enemies because he had too much love for himself. It led him to ruin. It will happen to us, too, if we allow it. Instead, surrender to God, mortify the flesh, and truly love others.

> *Search me, O God, and know my heart: try me, and know my thoughts: And see if there be any wicked way in me, and lead me in the way everlasting.*
> —Ps. 139:23–24

Factors to Consider

1. What do you want most out of life?

2. Think about your relationships. How would you rank them—poor, good, great? Why do you rank your relationships that way?

3. What can you do today to help repair a broken relationship in your life?

4. How has pride kept you from repairing a broken relationship?

5. Delusions of grandeur are dangerous. So is poor self-esteem. How would you describe your self-esteem today?

Factor Three:
Doubts of God

And straightway the father of the child cried out, and said with tears, LORD, *I believe; help thou mine unbelief.*

—Mark 9:24

Pharaoh was a man of faith.

It is true. That was established in the last chapter. Pharaoh's problem was that he placed his faith in the wrong things. The Egyptians were obviously a religious people. They believed in gods and had gods for just about everything. In his delusions of grandeur, Pharaoh probably believed he was the god of Egypt and of the Nile. Perhaps because he already believed in the supernatural, Pharaoh did not doubt the existence of the God of Moses and the Hebrews. However, he did not believe that Yahweh was to be feared or respected. So it is not that Pharaoh did not believe in God. He just doubted that God was the one true God and that the Hebrews were his chosen people.

And Pharaoh said, Who is the Lord, that I should obey his voice to let Israel go? I know not the Lord, neither will I let Israel go.

—Exod. 5:2

From the very beginning of this contest, Pharaoh's heart was hardened against God and God's people. Therefore, when the supernatural plagues began, Pharaoh was already firmly established and entrenched in a position of doubt. When Moses and Aaron asked Pharaoh to let them leave, he adamantly refused to let them go.

He had doubts of God.

What is doubt? Is it the same as unbelief? Close, but not exactly. Doubt is something that lurks in the shadows, hiding within the dark corners and edges of our faith. God's presence was revealed through the supernatural plagues that fell upon Egypt. Therefore, there was no point in denying God. He was there. Pharaoh saw it firsthand and witnessed the awesome wonders of God. However, he still doubted that God was who he said he was. In other words, Pharaoh doubted God's word. That was a major mistake.

Although we may believe in Jesus, our doubts can also ultimately lead to unbelief. Pharaoh obviously believed God existed. However, he doubted what God said. And that led him down a path of destruction. Left unchecked, our doubts of God will also lead to our undoing.

Pharaoh's Beliefs and Doubts

Although Pharaoh may have believed that he was a deity, he quickly learned that God Almighty had a presence in Egypt. In fact, God's power was very strong. He demonstrated it with Aaron's rod, which became a serpent, devouring the rods of Pharaoh's magicians, which also became serpents. It did not matter, though. Pharaoh still doubted God's word. As a result, God sent plagues upon Egypt to show Pharaoh a thing or two—or 10. To start things off, God said this to Moses:

> And the LORD spake unto Moses, Say unto Aaron, Take thy rod, and stretch out thine hand upon the waters of Egypt, upon their streams, upon their rivers, and upon their ponds, and upon all their pools of water, that they may become blood; and that there may be blood throughout all the land of Egypt, both in vessels of wood, and in vessels of stone.
>
> —Exod. 7:19

Imagine the stench! Wildlife, including fish, would have died. The smell of death would have permeated everything. Not only did the water of the Nile turn to blood, but standing water everywhere, including pots and jars, was affected. The Nile was considered the lifeblood of the Egyptians. God, with an ironic twist, supernaturally demonstrated his preeminence by turning its waters into actual blood. However, Pharaoh's magicians were able to reproduce this miracle by using their enchantments, so Pharaoh's doubts lingered. He was not convinced. The power of God was explained away. It was a trick. It was no big deal. Therefore, he hardened his heart and refused the request of Moses and Aaron. The Hebrews were going nowhere.

Unfortunately for Pharaoh, the contest did not stop there. This was only the beginning. The plague of blood was followed by another plague. God filled the Nile River with frogs. But that was not all. Frogs also covered the land. They hopped into Pharaoh's palace. They hopped into homes and beds. They even were found in the Egyptians' kneading bowls. Frogs were everywhere.

Somehow, the magicians were also able to duplicate this plague. Why would they want to do this? It must have seemed like a good idea to somebody at the time. Perhaps they did not think there were enough frogs already. Whatever the case, it was far beyond tolerable.

So Pharaoh called for Moses and Aaron and toad them—I mean, *told* them—to pray to God and ask him to remove the frogs. Why would he tell Moses and Aaron to do that? Well, because there were just way too many frogs. It was a no-brainer. But more importantly, and more seriously, it must have been because he had a measure of faith. He was not willing to obey God, but he acknowledged his existence, especially when things got bad.

Do you know anyone like that? We probably see this type of attitude toward God every day. Many believe there is a God but refuse to obey him. They have many doubts. They blame Him for all the bad things in life and call on him only to get out of trouble. They bargain with God. They try to make deals. Once their trouble is finally behind them, they move on and forget about God completely—until the next tragedy.

Moses did as Pharaoh instructed, and sure enough, the plague ended. The frogs—well, they croaked. Dead frogs piled up in heaps, and once again, there was an awful stench throughout the land. Pharaoh, in an act of narcissism, hardened his heart and rescinded his promise to let the Hebrews go. His actions proved he believed in God, but he still had doubts. He did not know God personally, and he certainly did not believe what God said. While round two ended in a standoff, Pharaoh's spiraling descent of doubt continued.

The third plague that confirmed God's presence was the plague of lice. These tiny little critters filled the air, covered men and animals, and appeared as a fine dust upon the land. This time, Pharaoh's magicians could not duplicate the plague. They even confessed to Pharaoh, "Then the magicians said unto Pharaoh, This is the finger of God: and Pharaoh's heart was hardened, and he hearkened not unto them; as the Lord had said" (Exod. 8:19).

These three plagues—blood, frogs, and lice—confirmed God's presence in Egypt. And they were just from his finger. What would happen if all of God showed up? The Egyptians were starting to get it. God proved he had power over the Egyptian gods and magicians.

Pharaoh, as evidenced by his actions, recognized that, too. However, he refused to completely apply it. Somewhere in the dark recesses of his faith, his doubts of God grew, and they overwhelmed him.

Likewise, we can find ourselves in similar situations. We may know that God exists, but we are not always sure he is with us. We may even cry out, "God, are you there?" And when God shows up and proves himself, we quickly return to our normal life and way of thinking, doubting God.

Practical Application

So what exactly is doubt? Contrary to what some may think, doubt is not the same as complete unbelief. The Jewish leaders who came up against Jesus were unbelievers. John 10:26 says, "But ye believe not, because ye are not of my sheep, as I said unto you."

In comparison, the father of the man in Mark 9:24 was not a full unbeliever. He was a doubter. Peter also shows us the difference between an unbeliever and a doubter. Remember when Peter walked on the water with Jesus and then began to sink? Jesus said to him, "O thou of little faith, wherefore didst thou doubt?" (Matt. 14:31).

As this verse shows, doubt is not the complete absence of faith. Peter had faith. It was small, but he had it. He actually walked on water. That took faith. Doubt, then, is faith that has somehow been burdened. It is usually caused by what we see in the natural. That is what happened to Peter, and as a result, he allowed himself to be pulled in two directions. Faith allowed him to walk on water, but doubt caused him to sink. He was, in other words, double-minded and, therefore, unstable.

> But let him ask in faith, nothing wavering. For he that wavereth is like a wave of the sea driven with the wind and tossed. For let not that man think that he shall receive any thing of the LORD. A double minded man is unstable in all his ways.
> —James 1:6–8

Doubt caused Peter to vacillate between two positions. With his eyes on Jesus, he could walk on water. With his eyes on the wind and waves, he would sink. It is, of course, impossible to go two directions at the same time. Therefore, faith and doubt represent a fork in the road. Doubt is an off-ramp from the highway of faith. Which direction will you go? Which path will you choose?

If the weight of doubt is not set aside, it will cause us to sink into unbelief. Peter learned this lesson. Pharaoh did not. Pharaoh chose the path of doubt over the path of faith. That is why Jesus responded differently to sincere doubters than He did to outright unbelievers. The longer we carry these doubts of God, the stronger their power becomes—even to the point of moving to the place of complete and utter unbelief. If that happens, we will sink.

Pharaoh could not lay aside these doubts of God, and his army sank to the bottom of the Red Sea. The conclusion of his doubt was destruction. So if doubt is that dangerous (and it is), how do we get rid of it? There are two steps that will help us overcome our doubts of God—repent and believe.

> *And saying, The time is fulfilled, and the kingdom of God is at hand: repent ye, and believe the gospel.*
> —Mark 1:15

Call it what it is: Doubt is a distrust of God and his word. Therefore, we must treat it as we would any other sin or any other weight that negatively affects our faith. Lay it aside. We must repent.

Repentance is more than just naming our struggle. Repentance is turning away from that struggle. Stop doubting God. Turn from it. Run from it. Run to God.

And believe. But consider poor Thomas. Whenever the topic of doubt comes up, his name probably rises to the top—doubting Thomas. He doubted once, and look what happened. He is branded for all time. Ouch! But notice Jesus's response. Thomas is not a full-fledged unbeliever. He is not like the Jewish leaders. He is not like Pharaoh. He is at a fork in the road. Will Thomas take the exit of doubt on the highway of faith? Or will he continue on his faith walk? Instead of a blistering rebuke, Jesus administers exactly what Thomas needed—a gentle yet firm rebuke, calling him to stop disbelieving. Thomas needed to take the path of faith. John 20:27 records this exchange:

> *Then saith he to Thomas, Reach hither thy finger, and behold my hands; and reach hither thy hand, and thrust it into my side: and be not faithless, but believing.*

Believing is perhaps easier than we often want to make it. Yes, wrestling with doubts can be a real struggle. But we can be victorious. There is a way to overcome. Spend time in the word of God. Read the Gospels, specifically the Gospel of John. The whole book is about believing. As John 20:31 says, it is the very reason the book was written.

And then we can talk about our doubts with close, trusted believers. Have them pray with you and for you. Encourage one another. Stand in the gap for one another. Fight for one another. Do not hide lingering doubts because of selfish pride. That will only lead to destruction.

Pharaoh neither repented nor believed. The cost was more than he could bear. His fall was great and impacted everyone around him. It is true that doubts do arise, sometimes to people of faith. But doubts limit the power of God in our lives. Dealing with them immediately and trusting God is of upmost importance.

Without doubt, the path is sure.

> *Trust in the* LORD *with all thine heart; and lean not unto thine own understanding. In all thy ways acknowledge him, and he shall direct thy paths.*
> —Prov. 3:5–6

Factors to Consider

1. Have you ever doubted God's word? Explain your response.

2. In your own words, describe what doubt looks like in your life. How does it play out in your thoughts, actions, and behaviors?

3. How do you determine whether to stay on the highway of faith or take the off-ramp of doubt? What influences your decisions?

4. Define repentance.

5. How do you deal with your own doubts of God?

Factor Four:
Deformity of Godliness

Having a form of godliness, but denying the power thereof: from such turn away.

—2 Tim. 3:5

Pharaoh would not concede defeat.

The first three plagues had a devastating effect on Egypt. The blood, the frogs, and the lice took their toll. Pharaoh, through his magicians, went toe-to-toe with God (or finger-to-finger, according to Exodus 8:19). Although we do not know Pharaoh's name, the apostle Paul calls the magicians by name in 2 Timothy 3:8: "Now as Jannes and Jambres withstood Moses, so do these also resist the truth: men of corrupt minds, reprobate concerning the faith."

This is the only place in canonical scripture that reveals their actual names. It could be a reference to a book of the Apocrypha called the Book of Jasher. This hidden book is also known as the Book of the Upright or the Book of the Just Man. It is referenced in Joshua 10:13 and again in 2 Samuel 1:18. Perhaps it was in this hidden book where Paul learned their names as he studied to be a Pharisee. He used them as an example in his second letter to Timothy as a warning of what to expect in the last days. Reading this chapter denotes perilous times—perilous times, indeed.

It was perilous under Pharaoh, too. Jannes and Jambres resisted the truth. They had some power. They used enchantments. They had a form of godliness. But it was not enough. It was not even close. After they were unable to compete with the third plague, they tapped out. They were done. In this contest, Pharaoh had to continue on his own. Still, he was convinced he was up to the challenge.

Without his magicians, Pharaoh had to use his own prowess. He was Pharaoh. He was the god-king. But there was only one way he could make this work. Somehow, he had to convince Moses that compromise was the answer. And he would set the example. Pharaoh would compromise by formally recognizing God but only if Moses would compromise God's command. Surely this would be a win-win situation. Right?

Fortunately, Moses understood that a form of godliness is not enough. Pharaoh's proposal for compromise would lead to only one thing—a lose-lose situation for everyone. And that is never right.

Pharaoh's Deformity of Godliness

After Jannes and Jambres left the competition, Pharaoh continued to harden his heart. The next series of plagues started, and a noticeable shift in the dynamics occurred. Starting with the plague of flies, the Lord put a division between the Hebrews and the Egyptians. In other words, the plagues that had previously impacted everyone in the land of Egypt would no longer impact God's people. Here is what God said.

> And I will sever in that day the land of Goshen, in which my people dwell, that no swarms of flies shall be there; to the end thou mayest know that I am the LORD in the midst of the earth.
>
> —Exod. 8:22

It happened just as God told Moses. Flies corrupted the land, except in Goshen. It was after this fourth plague that Pharaoh offered his first proposal. He could not count on his magicians, so he tried to be shrewd. He must have thought he could negotiate his way out of this mess. He told Moses and Aaron, "Go ye, sacrifice to your God in the land" (Exod. 8:25). In other words, Pharaoh told Moses and Aaron they could worship God, but they had to do it in Egypt. He offered a compromise.

Moses, however, knew that complete obedience to God was necessary. There was no room for compromise. Besides, Moses knew that if they worshiped God in Egypt, they would incur the Egyptian death penalty (Exod. 8:26). Moses responded.

We will go three days' journey into the wilderness, and sacrifice to the LORD our God, as he shall command us.
—Exod. 8:27

All righty then. That did not work. So Pharaoh offered his second proposal. He allowed them to go, but not very far (Exod. 8:28). Pharaoh tried this gambit to convince Moses and Israel that they were free, but Pharaoh would actually still have them within his grasp. Pharaoh was only granting a partial release—a form of godliness. It looked good, but there was no substance. Moses steadfastly refused to compromise. Nevertheless, the plague was lifted, and the flies departed. Pharaoh hardened his heart, and the contest continued.

Next, Moses warned Pharaoh that the Egyptians' livestock would die. Moses told Pharaoh exactly when it would happen—the very next day. That was the fifth plague. Once again, God's people were protected. It happened just as God said, and Pharaoh again hardened his heart. He would not relent.

His stubbornness brought on the sixth plague, which came without any warning or dialogue between Moses and Pharaoh. Moses simply took ashes and sprinkled them up toward heaven, and boils appeared on all the Egyptians. As one might guess, Pharaoh hardened his heart.

Moses then approached Pharaoh and warned him of coming hail. Even with this warning, Pharaoh did not obey. Hail with fire pummeled the land of Egypt. It killed anyone out in the field, including their animals. It destroyed crops. It damaged trees. And there was no hail in the land of Goshen. God, once again, spared his people.

In response, Pharaoh promised to let the Hebrews go. However, it was a lie. He was dealing deceitfully. For as soon as the hail stopped, Pharaoh sinned more. He hardened his heart. He would not let Israel go.

So God told Moses to warn Pharaoh about the next plague—the plague of locusts. This was the eighth plague. After a series of plagues with zero negotiations and one straight-up lie, Pharaoh tried his third proposal in an attempt to avoid this plague. His proposal was to release only the Hebrew males, but the women and children would be detained in Egypt. Pharaoh tried to convince Moses that the women and children were not important in the worship of God.

> Not so: go now ye that are men, and serve the LORD;
> for that ye did desire. And they were driven out from
> Pharaoh's presence.
> —Exod. 10:11

Pharaoh knew he would still have control if the women and children were excluded. Such a situation would cause divided attention and affection. Moses, of course, would not compromise. Therefore, the locusts descended on Egypt. They were everywhere. They ate everything. It was grievous. Pharaoh feigned repentance in order to stop the madness. True to his form, he hardened his heart, which led to the ninth plague and Pharaoh's final negotiation trick.

With the ninth plague, darkness fell. The Egyptians experienced three days of complete and utter darkness. Yet somehow, all the Hebrews had light in their homes. Pharaoh, in one last attempt, offered to let them go—on one condition. They had to leave their flocks and herds behind.

While plausible on the surface, there would have been serious consequences if Moses had agreed to this. First, they needed the animals for their sacrifices. They needed them for their worship. Without them, they would not have been obedient to God. Second, without their belongings, Israel would have been tempted to look back. No, this was not a viable condition. Moses responded to Pharaoh.

> *Our cattle also shall go with us; there shall not an*
> *hoof be left behind; for thereof must we take to serve*
> *the LORD our God; and we know not with what we*
> *must serve the LORD, until we come thither.*
>
> —Exod. 10:26

This, of course, was not acceptable to Pharaoh, and the face-to-face confrontation was finally over. Moses did not see him again. However, the contest between Pharaoh and God was not over. The setup for the final plague was in place. And it was all because Pharaoh wanted to compromise. He wanted just a form of godliness.

Practical Application

What is a form of godliness? In basic terms, it is empty religion. It is hypocrisy. It is a show. It is having the look but no power to back it up. It is like impersonating a police officer. You may look official, but you will end up getting in big trouble because you have no authority.

The root problem of empty religion is misplaced affection. Pharaoh's proposals were attempts to get Israel to have divided or misplaced affection. Had this occurred, Israel would have fallen into the trap of being lovers of themselves, lovers of material things, and lovers of pleasure rather than lovers of God. Paul described this condition in his letter to Timothy.

> *For men shall be lovers of their own selves, covetous, boasters, proud, blasphemers, disobedient to parents, unthankful, unholy, Without natural affection, truce-breakers, false accusers, incontinent, fierce, despisers of those that are good, Traitors, heady, highminded, lovers of pleasures more than lovers of God.*
>
> —2 Tim. 3:2–4

Pharaoh's first proposal was, "Go ye, sacrifice to your God in the land" (Exod. 8:25). There was no way Israel would be able to please Pharaoh and God at the same time. Likewise, we cannot serve two masters. Here is what Jesus taught.

> *No man can serve two masters: for either he will hate the one, and love the other; or else he will hold to the one, and despise the other. Ye cannot serve God and mammon.*
>
> —Matt. 6:24

Make no mistake. Satan wants full control of our lives. However, if he cannot have full control, he will settle for partial control. He realizes that partial control still keeps us within his jurisdiction. Pharaoh wanted Israel within his jurisdiction so he could control them. Likewise, we must have no compromise with evil. We cannot give it any place within our lives. We must get out of Egypt. Although Satan will settle for partial control, God will not.

Pharaoh's second proposal was that "only ye shall not go very far away" (Exod. 8:28). Pharaoh was only granting a partial release. He wanted the Israelites to still be within his grasp. God, however, demands all or nothing. We are commanded to love God entirely.

Like Paul, we must count all things loss for Christ. Unfortunately, some professing Christians have just enough religion to make them miserable. They remain within easy reach of Satan, and they do not totally refuse him. Christians must give no place to the devil.

> *Submit yourselves therefore to God. Resist the devil,*
> *and he will flee from you.*
>
> —James 4:7

Pharaoh's third proposal was for only the men to go (Exod. 10:11). Pharaoh did not believe that children were important in the worship of God, and he tried to convince Moses to believe the same way. Unfortunately, many people today do not think that children should be included in worship. In fact, many believe that children should be kept from it until they are old enough to make their own decisions. This, of course, is contrary to God's word.

> *And, ye fathers, provoke not your children to wrath:*
> *but bring them up in the nurture and admonition of*
> *the LORD.*
>
> —Eph. 6:4

Pharaoh's final proposal was "Go ... only let your flocks and herds be stayed" (Exod. 10:24). Leaving their animals would have caused a looking-back condition. Looking back, according to Jesus, is extremely problematic.

> *Remember Lot's wife.*
>
> —Luke 17:32

> *And Jesus said unto him, No man, having put his*
> *hand to the plough, and looking back, is fit for the*
> *kingdom of God.*
>
> —Luke 9:62

A divided heart will cause many to stumble. While some compromises may appear to be innocent, they can often involve more than what may appear on the surface. Pharaoh was relentless and willing to compromise. His offers may have been appealing, and some of them may have even appeared fair. However, any compromise would have impacted Israel's ability to worship God.

The same is true in our lives. Compromise will negatively affect our worship. It will cause us to have a form of godliness but without the power. That kind of condition does not foster a proper relationship with God.

Pharaoh was willing to compromise to get out of the afflictions of the plagues. In contrast, Moses was not willing to compromise. Pharaoh chose partial obedience, which is really a deformity of godliness. Moses obeyed completely. Moses chose godliness.

What will you choose?

Choosing rather to suffer affliction with the people of God, than to enjoy the pleasures of sin for a season.
—Heb. 11:25

Factors to Consider

1. What is a hypocrite?

2. Name a time when you compromised God's word. What was the result?

3. How are children involved in worship in your home? Your church?

4. Is there anything in life that causes you to want to look back and desire the things of the world? If so, what is it? How will you deal with the temptation to look back?

5. Resisting the devil can only come after submitting to God. How do you submit to God every day?

Factor Five:
Devoid of Guilt

For godly sorrow worketh repentance to salvation not to be repented of: but the sorrow of the world worketh death.

—2 Cor. 7:10

Pharaoh was sorry.

Well, sort of. He was sorry that this situation with the Hebrews was getting so out of hand that it began to negatively affect him and his life. It was getting too personal. His ego, his personality, could not deal with that. He needed this to stop. He needed this to stop—now. So he would say anything he needed to say. He would do anything he needed to do. However, any sorrow he displayed, like most things in his life, was merely for show. It was feigned. Unfortunately, Pharaoh seemed to have a complete lack of empathy, conscience, remorse, and shame.

He was devoid of guilt.

This is worldly sorrow, as Paul described to the Corinthian church. It is not actual sorrow for sinning. It is not doing an about-face and turning from sin. It is simply sorrow for getting caught.

It is sorrow that there are consequences to actions. The façade on the outside of Pharaoh had little or no resemblance to the reality of what was happening on the inside. But God knew. Because Pharaoh had no fear of the Lord, he also did not care what others thought of him. That allowed him to do and say the most outrageous things, completely ignore his own promises, and then continue to act as though nothing ever happened.

In other words, Pharaoh hardened his own heart. Then God also hardened Pharaoh's heart. It was a vicious cycle. What he chose to do on his own became his own punishment. We will look at this more in a later chapter. For now, it is important to understand that when you break it down, Pharaoh really only thought of himself. He did not care about or have empathy for others. He simply had his own agenda, and it did not matter that it was completely opposite of what God commanded.

That was a problem for Pharaoh because he was used to getting his way. If he wanted something, he made sure he got it by whatever means necessary. He manipulated. He deceived. He tried to give a false impression of who he really was to Moses in order to get what he wanted. However, Moses could see right through him.

> Let not Pharaoh deal deceitfully any more in not
> letting the people go to sacrifice to the LORD.
> —Exod. 8:29

Pharaoh's Lack of True Repentance

The first time Pharaoh seemed to have a change of heart was after the hailstorm. The hail, mingled with fire, was grievous to Egypt. It was devastating. Pharaoh would do anything to make these plagues stop. He tried being firm. That did not work. He tried negotiating. That did not work, either. He even tried ignoring and lying. Nothing worked. Pharaoh had just about enough, so it was time to take this contest to the next level. It was time to bring out the big guns.

And Pharaoh sent, and called for Moses and Aaron,
and said unto them, I have sinned this time: the LORD
is righteous, and I and my people are wicked.

—Exod. 9:27

Wait! What? Who saw that coming? Pharaoh admitted he was wrong? Yeah, not so fast. While most people feel regret or shame when they do something that hurts somebody, Pharaoh did not. No, he did not experience those types of feelings at all. He only experienced regret because his actions negatively affected his own life. Notice that Pharaoh said, "I have sinned this time." Uh, hello! This was the seventh plague. What about the other six times? Yeah, what about that, Pharaoh?

Unfortunately, Pharaoh was not truly sorry for the pain he had caused in the past. He was simply sorry for his own loss he was feeling right now. He must have figured that admitting his sin would shut Moses down and maybe even cause Moses to rethink how he felt about him. Perhaps he was trying to disarm Moses by completely catching him off guard. Admitting his own sin just might have silenced Moses and caused Moses to see that Pharaoh was really a nice guy after all. Maybe Moses would just call this whole silly nonsense off, right? Wrong. Here is what Moses said.

But as for thee and thy servants, I know that ye will
not yet fear the LORD God.

—Exod. 9:30

And Moses was absolutely right. He hit the nail on the head. Pharaoh hardened his heart and went right back to sinning. Rather than thinking about the impact of his actions on others, Pharaoh only thought about how his actions would get him what he wanted. Pharaoh simply saw Moses as an instrument to be used to get his way. Although Moses saw right through him, Pharaoh did get what he was asking for. The plague stopped. However, the downward cycle continued.

As we already saw, the next plague brought locusts. So what did Pharaoh do? He did the same thing that worked before. Why wouldn't he? He acted like he was sorry, but this time, he took it to another level.

> *Then Pharaoh called for Moses and Aaron in haste; and he said, I have sinned against the* LORD *your God, and against you. Now therefore forgive, I pray thee, my sin only this once, and intreat the* LORD *your God, that he may take away from me this death only.*
> —Exod. 10:16–17

The person who is devoid of guilt will apologize and seemingly repent, but only if you have something they need. However, once the heat is off, they will repeat the same pattern again and again and again. And notice how Pharaoh played on Moses's conscience. He actually asked for Moses's forgiveness. He counted on Moses's moral responsibility to get what he wanted by deflecting the responsibility of his own actions onto Moses. That is actually kind of brilliant. Manipulative, but brilliant. Well, at least it was effective for Pharaoh in the short term.

Pharaoh was too caught up in the moment to look long term, which is what really mattered. Short-term thinking yields short-term results. By thinking of his immediate needs, he only feigned repentance. Within a short period of time, the same pattern repeated itself. He was not dictated by others but by his own needs and wants. It is possible that when he made the promise, he had convinced himself he was genuine. And on some level, maybe he was sincere. Nevertheless, when the temptation to repeat the behavior resurfaced, he slipped back into his normal routine. This occurred round after round, until it finally ended in destruction.

Because Pharaoh did not think of long-term consequences, he did not plan ahead. He did not change. His patterns of behavior continually repeated. It was not a case of *if* it would happen again. It was a case of *when* it would happen again. Even after the death of his own firstborn, it was just a matter of time until the behavior repeated itself, and he was off to recapture the Hebrews.

Unfortunately for Pharaoh, he went down in spectacular fashion. And it was all because he was devoid of guilt and did not possess godly sorrow. He did not repent.

Practical Application

When reading these types of stories or studying characters with such extreme personality disorders, it is often tempting to see these same traits in others. Instead of self-examination, which can be painful, it is easier to identify faults in others. Perhaps that is why Jesus asked this:

> *And why beholdest thou the mote that is in thy brother's eye, but considerest not the beam that is in thine own eye?*
>
> —Matt. 7:3

We sometimes have big things in our own lives that need to be corrected. Instead, we find it easier to criticize the small things in others. Pharaoh had some big problems. So does each one of us. We need to start tossing out some beams. How do we do this?

There are other examples in scripture that are similar to Pharaoh's story. Fortunately, the failures of some individuals are juxtaposed with the successes of others. Individuals in similar situations deal with sorrow in different ways. The way they do it teaches us an important lesson about how we can act (or react) in various situations.

Consider King Saul and King David.

King Saul had conquered the Amalekites. However, after doing so, he disobeyed the Lord's instructions and spared their king and the choicest of their flocks and herds. The prophet Samuel then confronted Saul about this error. But instead of repenting, Saul made excuses. He insisted that he had obeyed the Lord. He then shifted the blame. He claimed that saving the flocks for sacrifice to the Lord was the people's idea. Then Samuel uttered these often-quoted words:

> *Behold, to obey is better than sacrifice, and to hearken than the fat of rams.*
>
> —1 Sam. 15:22

In 1 Samuel 15:24, King Saul finally admitted to the prophet that he had sinned. But he also asked to be honored in the sight of his elders (1 Sam. 15:30). In other words, he wanted to avoid public reproach. He wanted his reputation to remain intact. He confessed his sin but remained selfish. Outward appearances mattered too much to him.

In contrast, when King David was confronted by the prophet Nathan over his sin, his reaction was dramatically different. His sin was grievous and arguably even worse than King Saul's sin. King David had committed adultery with a married woman and then arranged the death of her husband as a cover-up. That seems pretty awful. However, when his sins were revealed, David became undone.

> *I have sinned against the LORD. And Nathan said unto David, The LORD also hath put away thy sin; thou shalt not die.*
>
> —2 Sam. 12:13

So, what is the difference between King Saul and King David? King David not only said the words of repentance, but his actions showed his true heart. He cried out to the Lord, fasted, and lay on the ground day and night for seven days, pleading for the life of his infant son. See the difference? King David was not concerned about himself. He really did not even care what others thought. He repented and grieved before God about the effect his sin had on others.

King Saul had worldly sorrow. King David had godly sorrow. One is completely selfish and cares only about the personal cost and effect of sin. The other is sorrowful before God and sincerely cares about offending him. But it does not stop there. Godly sorrow is concerned about the impact of the sin on others.

Now consider Judas and Peter.

On the night before the crucifixion, one of Jesus's disciples betrayed him, and one denied him. Both of these sins were against Jesus directly. The Bible records how both Judas and Peter responded. Scripture tells us that Judas repented.

> *Then Judas, which had betrayed him, when he saw that he was condemned, repented himself, and brought again the thirty pieces of silver to the chief priests and elders.*
>
> —Matt. 27:3

Unfortunately, Judas's regret and remorse were completely self-centered. He was sorrowful, but not so much for the plight of Jesus as he was for himself. He felt bad that he felt bad. Therefore, he was really only sorry for himself. He did not change his mind and behavior for the better because he hated his sin. Instead, he went out and hanged himself. He had worldly sorrow. He hated himself instead of hating his sin.

Peter, on the other hand, went out and wept bitterly after denying Christ. Was his sorrow godly or worldly? His actions tell the story. While Judas immediately went out and hanged himself, Peter returned to the disciples. When he heard word of Jesus's resurrection, he went in search of the Lord, even though he had sinned against him. As a result, Peter was ultimately restored. He turned from his sin.

Judas's sorrow led to death. Peter's led to life. That is the difference between worldly sorrow and godly sorrow. King David and Peter were both guilty. Yet they trusted in the Lord. That act of faith took away their guilt and shame. Pharaoh, King Saul, and Judas were devoid of guilt when they were, in fact, as guilty as sin. They thought their actions were right. When confronted, they justified themselves in their own eyes and did not repent with godly sorrow. And that led to their destruction.

What kind of sorrow do you have?

There is a way that seemeth right unto a man, but the end thereof are the ways of death.

—Prov. 16:25

Factors to Consider

1. How do you respond when you get caught sinning?

2. Describe the difference between godly sorrow and worldly sorrow.

3. Have you ever apologized just so you could get out of trouble? If so, did it work? Why or why not?

4. What is the sign of true repentance?

5. Why is it easier to see problems in others and not so easy to see them in yourself? How do you fix that?

Factor Six:
Decisions of Greed

For what shall it profit a man, if he shall gain the whole world, and lose his own soul?

—Mark 8:36

Pharaoh made a final decision—a very bad final decision. The Lord told Moses that one last plague would come to Pharaoh and all of Egypt. For Pharaoh, it would be the so-called straw that broke the camel's back. God told Moses that after this plague, Pharaoh would let them go. Not only would Pharaoh let them go, he would actually throw them out of Egypt. He would be eager to see them go. The Egyptian people would want them gone, too.

And he called for Moses and Aaron by night, and said, Rise up, and get you forth from among my people, both ye and the children of Israel; and go, serve the LORD, as ye have said. Also, take your flocks and your herds, as ye have said; and be gone; and bless me also.

And the Egyptians were urgent upon the people, that
they might send them out of the land in haste; for they
said, We be all dead men.

—Exod. 12:31–33

This time, there were no negotiations. No pleading. No bargaining. No deception. Just go. However, the little add-on at the end of his proclamation—"and bless me also"—is interesting. Sigh. Isn't that just like Pharaoh? He is constantly and relentlessly in it for himself. He just had to throw that in, too. He is absolutely exhausting. I am almost tired of studying him. Almost.

Anyway, after this final plague, the Hebrews left Egypt in a hurry, as instructed. And true to Pharaoh's character, he changed his mind. All he needed was a little time to revert right back to his true nature. Even after all the horrendous plagues he had endured, he questioned his decision. He probably said something like this: *Hold on. Wait. One. Minute. Why have I done this?* It just occurred to him that he had lost a lot of servants and slaves. That's no good. It is no good at all. He had to get them back. They were free labor. This transaction was costing him money.

He let greed influence his decision-making.

Greed is a sin that is often discussed in scripture and closely tied to covetousness, which is prohibited by the tenth commandment. Christian teachings have also included greed among the seven deadly sins: pride, greed, lust, envy, gluttony, wrath, and sloth. The idea is that these sins are extreme demonstrations (or abuses) of our natural passions. We all have them in some form or another. Yet left unchecked, they become sins when they begin to rule us. Committing these sins will then lead directly to other sins. That, of course, then leads to devastating consequences, for ourselves and others. Pharaoh learned that the hard way.

While the Ten Commandments are part of the Old Testament law, diligent study will reveal that the New Testament reinforces the importance of adherence to all of them. They include honoring the Sabbath, which is no longer a day but rather the rest we find in Christ. The Sabbath is another topic worthy of a separate study. Getting back to covetousness, Jesus said:

> And he said unto them, Take heed, and beware of covetousness: for a man's life consisteth not in the abundance of the things which he possesseth.
>
> —Luke 12:15

Oops. Pharaoh obviously missed this principle.

Pharaoh's Greedy Decision

The tenth and final plague on Egypt was the death of the firstborn. It would affect everyone from Pharaoh to the servants, to the people, and even to all the animals. The children of Israel, however, would be protected. As one could imagine, this plague would cause great sorrow across Egypt. Even after receiving a final warning, Pharaoh would not relent. His heart was hardened. He would not let the people of Israel go.

So God gave Moses instructions on how to institute Passover, which would protect the Israelites on the fateful night and also serve as a memorial for generations to come. Passover also serves as a typology of Christ, for he is our Passover lamb. During this ritual, the Hebrews were instructed to apply the blood of the lamb on the lintels and doorposts. In so doing, the destroyer would not visit their homes.

> For the LORD will pass through to smite the Egyptians; and when he seeth the blood upon the lintel, and on the two side posts, the LORD will pass over the door, and will not suffer the destroyer to come in unto your houses to smite you.
>
> —Exod. 12:23

Do you ever watch a movie and get excited when the title of the movie is actually said during the dialogue? I do. I am a little weird that way. I point it out every time it happens. I get just as excited when I read that part of Exodus 12:23 that says "the Lord will pass over the door." There! There it is! Passover! It is a wonderful example of the Lord's salvation. And that should excite us.

But for the Egyptians, it was not as exciting. It was a fearful thing. It was an awful night of death. It was not a pass over. It was a pass through. As God passed through, all of the firstborn in Egypt were killed, just as he had warned. Even Pharaoh's firstborn died. The firstborn of the cattle died. A great cry arose in Egypt, for there was not one house left unaffected. Enough was enough. Pharaoh was spent.

It was time to let Israel go. Or was it?

Pharaoh went ahead and ordered Israel to leave. So they left. But they did not leave empty-handed. They asked the Egyptians for silver and gold. They asked for clothing. The Egyptians wanted them gone so badly that they gave them whatever they wanted. Take it. Take it all. Just go! So Israel plundered Egypt while exiting. They were on their way out with nothing but clear skies and fair winds.

Well, not exactly clear skies. God led them out with a pillar of a cloud by day and a pillar of fire by night. These signs were to lead and protect the people, for God told Moses that Pharaoh was going to come after them. And sure enough, he did.

> *And it was told the king of Egypt that the people fled: and the heart of Pharaoh and of his servants was turned against the people, and they said, Why have we done this, that we have let Israel go from serving us? And he made ready his chariot, and took his people with him.*
>
> —Exod. 14:5–6

He made his final decision. He was going to recapture the Israelites. After all, not only did the Egyptians lose their free labor, they were also just plundered by the Israelites. They needed their stuff back. In a decision fueled by greed, Pharaoh chased after the Hebrews. He thought he had them boxed in. Moses must have appeared to be a poor general. It looked like a sure thing for Pharaoh. But God moved between the Egyptians and the Israelites and opened a way of escape through the Red Sea.

As Moses instructed, the children of Israel walked across the sea on dry ground. The waters of the sea became walls on both sides, creating a path straight across. In the face of this awesome miracle, Pharaoh still thought he had a chance. The hubris he displayed is mind-boggling. How he ever thought this was going to end well is unfathomable. And it does not end well. His final mistake is recorded in Exodus 14:23:

> *And the Egyptians pursued, and went in after them to the midst of the sea, even all Pharaoh's horses, his chariots, and his horsemen.*

Once the Israelites were safe on the other side, God caused the wheels of the Egyptians' chariots to fall off. In great fear and panic, the Egyptians tried to escape. They recognized that God was fighting for Israel. They had to turn back. But it was too late.

> *And the waters returned, and covered the chariots, and the horsemen, and all the host of Pharaoh that came into the sea after them; there remained not so much as one of them.*
>
> —Exod. 14:28

Pharaoh's greedy decision cost him his chariots and his prized horses. It also cost his army their very lives. Selfish decisions—greedy decisions—are like that. They do not just affect one person; they affect many. Therefore, we must take heed and be mindful of our own greediness.

Practical Application

How does this apply to us today?

Think of it like this. When the stock market falls, it is not unusual for investors to get discouraged or even nervous about their stocks. But they should not overreact. A fluctuating market is normal, and a volatile stock market is a characteristic of the economy. Disciplined investors factor this volatility into their long-term investment strategy. That helps them avoid making foolish decisions based on the fear of losing their investments in the short term. Greedy investors, on the other hand, make poor short-term decisions. They react, sometimes overreact, and it can cost them in the long run.

Now, when we see the rich lose money, we sometimes laugh at their calamity. We find it funny because we do not often see ourselves as actively storing up worldly treasures for ourselves. Somehow, we think this principle does not apply to us individually. It is a tragedy when we lose a $10 bill; it is hilarious when a billionaire loses millions of dollars. We often do not see the little glimpses of manifested greed in our own lives. If we are not careful, we can become more and more unaware that we are participants in a world system that will play on our basest instincts, including greed—especially greed. When we put our trust in material things, a fear of what the future may hold can shatter whatever feeble hope materialism brings.

When our trust is in material things, we often try building a bigger barn, stockpiling more provisions, and arming ourselves with more ways to protect our investments. This type of thinking can consume us. It may seem like a great idea. However, it can cause us to make decisions based on greed. Jesus addresses this in a parable found in Luke.

And he spake a parable unto them, saying, The ground of a certain rich man brought forth plentifully; And he thought within himself, saying, What shall I do, because I have no room where to bestow my fruits?

And he said, This will I do: I will pull down my barns, and build greater; and there will I bestow all my fruits and my goods. And I will say to my soul, Soul, thou hast much goods laid up for many years; take thine ease, eat, drink, and be merry. But God said unto him, Thou fool, this night thy soul shall be required of thee: then whose shall those things be, which thou has provided? So is he that layeth up treasure for himself, and is not rich toward God.

—Luke 12:16–21

Greed is an intense and selfish desire for something. Greed goes beyond money, chariots, horses, and land. Greed can cause us to think we are always right. Greed can cause us to want to be socially acceptable. Greed can cause us to check our phones relentlessly to see how many friends we have on social media or how many people "like" our posts. Greed can cause us to become so obsessed, wanting to protect ourselves and what we own at any cost. Greed can—and will—consume us, and it will ultimately destroy us.

Okay. That sounds bad. So what is the solution? The apostle Paul clearly lays it out in Colossians.

Mortify therefore your members which are upon the earth; fornication, uncleanness, inordinate affection, evil concupiscence, and covetousness, which is idolatry.

—Col. 3:5

We referred to this verse earlier in Factor Two. It is applicable here, too. Paul says we must put to death the things that are within us that are worldly. Covetousness, which some versions translate as greed in this verse, is exactly the same as idolatry. It is not a term we use much anymore since we think it is something from long ago. It is not something we practice now, or so we believe. We may have a false notion that idolatry has been put to death.

However, we are missing something extremely important if we think idolatry is only about pagan worship and images carved out of wood and stone. Idolatry is, in reality, alive and well today. Idols of financial security, idols of power and privilege, and idols of superiority are all created by our greed. Whenever we resort to unethical business practices in order to achieve a positive bottom line, we turn profit into an idol. Whenever we think that God only favors our nation because we are Americans and we make our nationality synonymous with Christianity, we turn our patriotism into an idol. Whenever we see other people as objects to be used or simply as a means to achieve whatever it is we desire, we turn those desires into an idol.

It is uncomfortable to think in these terms. Yet we must. We should constantly check our motivations. Are they selfish? Or are they selfless? It is important because all of our choices have real-world consequences. Beyond that, our choices also have real eternal consequences. That is why we must mortify the deeds of the flesh.

We must be vigilant. It is not that prosperity and success are wrong. Used correctly, they can be a way to give more. They can help us be good stewards of what God has graciously provided. However, if we put our faith and trust in material things, it will lead to greed and, ultimately, destruction—just as it did for Pharaoh.

> *Some trust in chariots, and some in horses: but we will remember the name of the LORD our God.*
> —Ps. 20:7

> *For the love of money is the root of all evil: which while some coveted after, they have erred from the faith, and pierced themselves through with many sorrows.*
> —1 Tim. 6:10

Ultimately, it comes down to a heart problem. Jesus made it clear that our hearts will be wherever we place our treasures. Pharaoh had his treasure in Egypt. He had his treasure in himself. Therefore, his heart was hardened to the things of God. He had a disposition of granite. We will study that next. Before we do, answer this one question, because it will tell you the location of your heart.

Where is my treasure?

> *But seek ye first the kingdom of God, and his righteousness; and all these things shall be added unto you.*
>
> —Matt. 6:33

Factors to Consider

1. What does greed look like in your life?

2. How do we "mortify" those things within us that are worldly?

3. Define idolatry.

4. Is money the root of all evil? If not, what is, and why is it a problem?

5. Where is your treasure?

Factor Seven:
Disposition of Granite

Yea, they made their hearts as an adamant stone,
lest they should hear the law, and the words which
the Lord of hosts hath sent in his spirit by the former
prophets: therefore came a great wrath from the Lord
of hosts.

—Zech. 7:12

Pharaoh had a heart condition.

His problem was not a physical one. It was spiritual. Throughout the story of the Exodus, we find that both divine-hardening and self-hardening occurred during this contest between Yahweh and Pharaoh. Below is a list of references where God said he would harden Pharaoh's heart, where God actually hardened Pharaoh's heart, where it is implied that God hardened Pharaoh's heart, where it is unknown who hardened Pharaoh's heart, and where Pharaoh hardened his own heart.

- Exodus 4:21   God declared he would harden Pharaoh's heart
- Exodus 7:3   God declared he would harden Pharaoh's heart
- Exodus 7:13   God hardened Pharaoh's heart
- Exodus 7:14   Implied God hardened Pharaoh's heart (restating of verse 13)
- Exodus 7:22   Unknown who hardened Pharaoh's heart
- Exodus 8:15   Pharaoh hardened his own heart
- Exodus 8:19   Unknown who hardened Pharaoh's heart
- Exodus 8:32   Pharaoh hardened his own heart
- Exodus 9:7   Unknown who hardened Pharaoh's heart
- Exodus 9:12   God hardened Pharaoh's heart
- Exodus 9:34   Pharaoh hardened his own heart
- Exodus 9:35   Implied Pharaoh hardened his own heart (restating of verse 34)
- Exodus 10:1   God hardened Pharaoh's heart
- Exodus 10:20 God hardened Pharaoh's heart
- Exodus 10:27 God hardened Pharaoh's heart
- Exodus 11:10 God hardened Pharaoh's heart
- Exodus 14:4   God declared he would harden Pharaoh's heart
- Exodus 14:5   Implied God hardened Pharaoh's heart (restating of verse 4)
- Exodus 14:8   God hardened Pharaoh's heart

Wow! That is a long list. As the sheer number of references to this condition in this story implies, the heart of the matter was, indeed, a matter of the heart—Pharaoh's heart. In the next chapter, we will discuss who was the ultimate cause of Pharaoh's hardening and whether it was a conditional judgment with respect to Pharaoh's own sin. For now, we are going to investigate what it means to have a hardened heart and what the solution is to this destructive spiritual condition.

It is important to understand this condition because it did not happen only to Pharaoh. Hebrews 3:7–11 tells us that the very children of Israel who witnessed this contest between Yahweh and Pharaoh first-hand later hardened their own hearts. As Zechariah 7:12 tells us, hundreds of years later, the people of Israel hardened their hearts toward God again. Throughout history, this phenomenon has occurred time and time again. It still does today. In response, God has graciously described this condition for us and has also given us the cure.

> *Wherefore (as the Holy Ghost saith, To day if ye will hear his voice, Harden not your hearts, as in the provocation, in the day of temptation in the wilderness: When your fathers tempted me, proved me, and saw my works forty years. Wherefore I was grieved with that generation, and said, They do always err in their heart; and they have not known my ways. So I sware in my wrath, They shall not enter into my rest.)*
> —Heb. 3:7–11

Pharaoh's Hardened Heart

As the list of scripture references in Exodus shows, Pharaoh clearly had this condition. If it was not a physical one, what was it? Throughout the ancient world, the heart was often referenced as the seat of intelligence and emotions within a person. As we know today, the heart of a person is not housed within the blood pump known as the heart; it resides in the brain. The heart-mind is an essential part of the makeup of human beings and is, I believe in this context, synonymous with a person's spirit. Since we are created in the image of God, we have three major components to our existence: body, soul, and spirit. Regarding the spirit, Proverbs 17:22 says, "A merry heart doeth good like a medicine: but a broken spirit drieth the bones."

Understanding how poetry works in the Old Testament will help us comprehend the parallelism in this verse and that the heart and the spirit are synonymous. The writer tells us that the emotional health of our spirit has a direct impact on the health of our physical bodies. Science today has proved what the Bible has told us for thousands of years. However, our spirit is not just our emotions. It is also our intellect. Proverbs 23:7 says, "For as he thinketh in his heart, so is he."

Thinking is intellect, not just an emotional response. Jesus taught us this:

> For from within, out of the heart of men, proceed evil thoughts, adulteries, fornications, murders, Thefts, covetousness, wickedness, deceit, lasciviousness, an evil eye, blasphemy, pride, foolishness: All these evil things come from within, and defile the man.
>
> —Mark 7:21–23

In other words, what we demonstrate in our behaviors and actions comes from the heart. We think about it. Then we do it. That occurs within the human brain.

Therefore, all sin begins in the heart of a person through emotional responses and thought processes. Do you want to stop sin at the source? Then you must submit your thought life (mind) to the Lord. You must submit your emotions (heart) to the Lord. Yes, you must yield your spirit (mind/heart) to his Holy Spirit.

We must worship him with everything that we are—body, soul, and spirit.

> And he answering said, Thou shalt love the LORD thy God with all thy heart, and with all thy soul, and with all thy strength, and with all thy mind; and thy neighbor as thyself.
>
> —Luke 10:27

But wait! This verse lists four things: heart, soul, strength, and mind. What is going on? While this verse looks like four things make up the essence of a person, understanding what we just learned (that the heart and mind both make up the spirit) clearly points to the body (physical), soul (life essence), and spirit (heart/mind). That is how we are to love the Lord, with everything that we are—body, soul, and spirit.

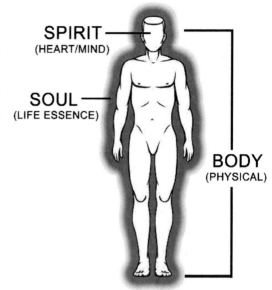

SPIRIT (HEART/MIND)

SOUL (LIFE ESSENCE)

BODY (PHYSICAL)

Now Pharaoh clearly was not loving Yahweh in any way at all. His spirit, his heart, and his mind were hardened against God. The only way he could have been cured from this condition was to submit to God's authority and obey God's word. As we learned in "Factor Three: Doubts of God," Pharaoh doubted that God was who he said he was. Pharaoh doubted God's word.

> *And Pharaoh said, Who is the LORD, that I should obey his voice to let Israel go? I know not the LORD, neither will I let Israel go.*
>
> —Exod. 5:2

His heart was hardened to God from the very beginning. The term *adamant stone* in Zechariah 7:12 is sometimes translated *flint stone*. You might say that Pharaoh was the original Flintstone (sorry, Fred). Instead of crying, "Yabba Dabba Doo!" Pharaoh cried, "Abba? Abba Who?" He did not know his heavenly father. He did not listen to his voice.

As a result, Pharaoh sat in judgment of God's word. He criticized God's word. He even challenged God's word. Does that sound familiar at all? If Pharaoh wanted to avoid a hardened heart and the consequences of his actions, he should have submitted to God's word. He should have listened to God's voice. But he did not.

The soul-destroying hardness of his heart eventually caught up with him. It also caught up with the children of Israel when God did not allow them to enter the Promised Land. Living with a hardened heart has serious ramifications. It will catch up with us, too.

It did with me.

Kevin's Hardened Heart

At the age of 15, I was diagnosed with a life-changing condition—psoriasis. I did not know it at the time, but this chronic condition would affect me for years to come. It still does today. However, dealing with a severe form of the disease during my pivotal teenage years caused me to harden my heart. It impacted my body. It impacted my self-esteem. It impacted my relationships both with God and others. I followed my heart, and it led me down a path I did not want to go. I could not find my way back.

Just a few years earlier, I had received the call of God on my life. It was at our summer youth camp, then called Circle J Ranch, which is now Bethel Youth Conference Center. I knew God was going to use me. I *knew* it. My passion and excitement for God swung high on the pendulum of emotions. But what I did not understand was how fickle my emotions could be. For when I truly realized the severity of my condition, my passion for God was just as intense, but it swung to the other side of the pendulum. My anger with God was as strong as my love for God.

Years of failed treatments, years of self-esteem issues, and years of hardening my heart kept me from listening to God's voice and serving him. Sure, I went through some of the motions, but it was just that—empty religion. I used the hardness of my heart to build a wall around my emotions. I did it to protect myself. What I originally planned as a place of protection within my heart very quickly became a cold, dark prison.

There was no escape.

Until God broke through and rescued me. It was about 11 years after my initial diagnosis. Life continued, but I had been slowly dying on the inside all those years. Then something happened with my treatments and my condition. I became very sick. Critically sick. To this day, I am unsure exactly what happened, but I ended up in the hospital not knowing if I would live or die. My skin became erythrodermic, turning red and peeling off in sheets. I couldn't eat. My heart was racing. I was in bad shape for nearly a month.

It was during that time when I was alone in my hospital bed with nothing to do but think that I reviewed my life. When my daughter, who was only five at the time, came to visit me, I thought, *If I die, what will my daughter remember about me? What kind of father had I been? What did I teach her about life, struggles, love, and God?* It was during those times of contemplation that God broke through my heart of stone. He got under my skin and into my heart. He showed up, and for the first time since I was diagnosed, I began to understand. I realized that his grace is sufficient for me—no matter what.

From that point forward, I began to let God use me in ministry. I took small steps at first. But I took them. I still struggled with the disease, but I had made my peace with God. It was not always easy, but he and I together handled it. Oh, we still had straightforward conversations about my condition. But I kept my heart open to his word. For a time, I even used my experiences and my faith to lead a support group for people struggling like I was.

Years later, I finally found a medicine that helped me control the disease. I was very thankful. I *am* very thankful. But then my daughter was also diagnosed with psoriasis. I had passed it on to her genetically. I was crushed when she was diagnosed. I could feel the edges of my heart hardening once again. I had to get it under control by listening to God's word. I did. And life went on.

Even as I am writing this book, my son was also diagnosed with psoriasis. At 14 years old, he is showing the same symptoms I did when I was close to that age. In the natural, it does not look good. Just a week before writing these very words, I was at the doctor's office with him. While waiting for the practitioner to return to the room, I apologized to my son. I felt guilty. I felt angry. Once again, I felt the edges of my heart begin to harden. I could feel it closing in, and I felt guilty that I had passed on this disease to both of my children. I said to my son, "I am so sorry that you have to deal with this." And then he said something to me that I will never forget. "If you can deal with it, I can, too."

And then it hit me. The calluses infringing on the edges of my heart dried up and crumbled away, leaving a heart of flesh. Tears gathered in the corners of my eyes. The very questions I asked myself in the hospital bed so many years ago made perfect sense again. A hardened heart did not just affect me and my relationship with God. It affected others, too. Likewise, a heart broken before Jesus did not just affect my relationship with God. It affected others, too.

No matter what we do, our lives serve as an example to others. What kind of example do you want to be for your children, your relatives, the children in your church, and the children in your neighborhood? Look, life happens to all of us. I get that. God allows circumstances to happen that we do not always understand or want. However, the way we respond during those times makes all the difference. It makes a difference now and also in the future.

So we must not give up. If we do, that is when we will truly fail. We must not give in to the circumstances of life. We must not let our hearts be hardened through the trials and tests we experience.

I wrote the following poem in 2012. Although somewhat melancholy in tone, it is meant to capture the seriousness of keeping our emotions and thoughts in check through the storms of life. We have a lot to watch over, and it sometimes feels like we are all alone. Sometimes, it feels like we have failed. Sometimes, it feels like God has failed us. He hasn't. Neither are we alone.

I stand motionless, like a stone
On the peak of a hill looking down
Over the cold gray world; all alone
Although surrounded by many in this town

My will is worn by wind and time
Yet still chiseled and set like granite
A form of who and what I once was; so sublime
Eyes glazed, focus lost—I don't understand it

For I once lived with hopes and dreams
But when these feelings are displayed and show
It is difficult to stem the tide and streams
Of happiness and sorrow and of joy and woe

So how does one learn to balance
The pendulum of swinging emotions wide
A variety of feelings by my spirit's allowance
It is hard to let go of failed visions I tried

Yet I am still a dreamer true
A sentinel standing but not alone on this hill
Alive in my dreams and not completely through
As long as I submit to God's perfect will

Personal Application

Yes, submitting to God's word is the key to overcoming a hardened heart. The only way for us to know God's plan is to listen and obey what he has revealed in scripture. Let's go back and review what happened to the children of Israel.

> *Wherefore (as the Holy Ghost saith, To day if ye will hear his voice, Harden not your hearts, as in the provocation, in the day of temptation in the wilderness:*

75

*When your fathers tempted me, proved me, and saw
my works forty years. Wherefore I was grieved with
that generation, and said, They do always err in their
heart; and they have not known my ways. So I sware
in my wrath, They shall not enter into my rest.)*

—Heb. 3:7–11

These people in the wilderness should have known God's ways, but they did not. Not really. Oh, they had it. They just did not apply it to their lives. Psalm 19 is one of my favorite psalms that teaches about submitting to God's word. In this psalm, the writer explains that nature tells us there is a God. However, nature does not give us his name. Then the writer switches gears and talks about God's word. He changes from using God's title (Elohim) to using God's personal name (Yahweh). In essence, he is saying that nature tells us there is a God but that God's word tells us who he is—by name.

Spending time with God while fishing, hiking, or hunting is good, but it is not good enough. Nature is amazing, and it does declare the glory of God. However, a wilderness adventure is not always all that it's cracked up to be. Just ask the children of Israel. The only way to truly know God is to spend time in his word.

We need to know God—personally. That means we must spend time in his word. We are responsible to learn and submit to God's ways. Psalm 19:11 says, "Moreover by them is thy servant warned: and in keeping of them there is great reward." We cannot plead ignorance since that is not a defense that will hold up. It did not work for the children of Israel in the wilderness. They should have known God's ways. It was given to them. Yet they hardened their hearts. And so we should learn God's ways before we find ourselves in difficult situations. His wisdom has been given to us, too. We have it. We need to use it and apply it. If we neglect wisdom when we have the opportunity to learn it, we will most likely find ourselves overwhelmed and hardened when we are in a crisis.

Unfortunately, many church people today do not like to take the time to actually study God's word. We like to have experiences instead. Don't get me wrong, I like experiences, too. I love it when God reveals his mighty power through miracles. However, miracles alone will not change a hardened heart, nor will they keep us from having one. We know that because the Israelites saw some of the greatest miracles ever performed while they were in the wilderness. They saw the 10 plagues. They walked across the Red Sea on dry ground. They ate the manna provided by God. Their shoes did not wear out. They witnessed God's wonders for 40 years. If miracles alone could soften hearts, the children of Israel would have been among the most faithful people in the history of the planet. But they were not.

I also mentioned this principle in my previous book, *The Elisha Factor,* because it is extremely important. Miracles will not convince us because we are not changed by the miraculous. We are changed by the message—the message of the cross. If we focus on miracles, we are easily discouraged when they fade away into a distant memory. If we focus on the message, we will be encouraged because God's word does not pass away. It stands forever. Here is what Jesus said.

> *And he said unto him, If they hear not Moses and the prophets, neither will they be persuaded, though one rose from the dead.*
>
> —Luke 16:31

Jesus was emphasizing the importance of his word. We often say, "Do it again, Lord, do it again," because we want a repeat of the experience. We say this because we may enjoy the experience more than the word. It is not because we question what God has done for us. We are just saying, "God, what have you done for us lately?" We follow after the signs and wonders when, in reality, signs and wonders should be following after us. We need to be doing something instead of expecting God to always do something for us. But when we focus on the miracle, we can become discouraged during times of extreme trials when there appear to be a lack of miracles. That is what happened to the children of Israel, and that is what happened to me.

I grumbled and complained. So did the children of Israel. They murmured against God. So did I. When we are confronted with life, we have the choice of submitting to him or grumbling and going back to the world. The apostle Paul demonstrated the proper response to these types of situations. He was in prison. Fellow Christian leaders criticized him. He could have easily complained about the unfair circumstances in his life. Who would have blamed him? Yet he wrote this:

> *Do all things without murmurings and disputings.*
> —Phil. 2:14

With the right attitude, our submission to and trust in God and his word will lead us into joy, even though we may find ourselves in the middle of unimaginable trials. An attitude of pride, self-centeredness, and grumbling will cause us to harden our hearts, resist God's ways, and turn back to the temporary pleasures of the world. Pharaoh had a choice. The children of Israel had a choice. We have a choice.

But here is a word of caution. Do not fall into the trap of believing that your trials are always due to your lack of faith or a result of your sin. The church is sometimes good at heaping condemnation on those who are experiencing difficult situations. That has happened to me a time or two. To be sure, we must have faith, and trials are a great time to use that faith. And sin does bring consequences. So, when trials happen, examine yourself, correct yourself where needed, but do not condemn yourself for your trials. We all have them. Paul was a great man of faith. And he also had trials.

> *And lest I should be exalted above measure through*
> *the abundance of the revelations, there was given to*
> *me a thorn in the flesh, the messenger of Satan to*

buffet me, lest I should be exalted above measure. For this thing I besought the LORD thrice, that it might depart from me. And he said unto me, My grace is sufficient for thee: for my strength is made perfect in weakness. Most gladly therefore will I rather glory in my infirmities, that the power of Christ may rest upon me. Therefore, I take pleasure in infirmities, in reproaches, in necessities, in persecutions, in distresses for Christ's sake: for when I am weak, then am I strong.

—2 Cor. 12:7–10

When we submit to God's word, we enter into his rest. His power rests upon us. God's rest to the children of Israel was a reference regarding the Promised Land. It also has a spiritual application to us today since God's rest is found in Jesus. That does not mean we do not have to work—after all, there were battles Israel had to fight in the Promised Land. But it does mean that we do not have to work for our salvation. There are spiritual battles we must fight today. However, God's rest comes to us when we believe him and submit to him, because he justifies the ungodly.

In other words, he gives us a new heart—a right spirit—when we ask him.

Create in me a clean heart, O God; and renew a right spirit within me.

—Ps. 51:10

And I will give them one heart, and I will put a new spirit within you; and I will take the stony heart out of their flesh and will give them an heart of flesh: That they may walk in my statutes, and keep mine ordinances, and do them: and they shall be my people, and I will be their God. But as for them whose heart

*walketh after the heart of their detestable things and
their abominations, I will recompense their way upon
their own heads, saith the LORD God.*

—Ezek. 11:19–21

Your heart is either hardening against God because you are
resisting his ways, or your heart is growing softer toward God because
you are submitting to his word. Your response to your trials reveals
your heart. It did for the children of Israel. It did for me.

It also revealed Pharaoh's hardened heart.

Factors to Consider

1. What are the three major components of our existence?

2. Where does sin begin? How does it happen?

3. How do we get to know God personally? Where is the best place to find out who he is?

4. Are trials always due to sin? Why or why not?

5. What is the answer to the condition of a hardened heart?

Factor Eight:
Destiny or Grace

For the scripture saith unto Pharaoh, Even for this same purpose have I raised thee up, that I might shew my power in thee, and that my name might be declared throughout all the earth.

—Rom. 9:17

Pharaoh lost. Big time.

But did he have to lose? Was it a foregone conclusion? Did God just set him up to be used and tossed aside with no thought or concern about him individually? These are the difficult questions. In response, many debates about the will of God and the will of humans have occurred over the centuries. Indeed, sadly, these debates (among others, of course) have split churches, created multiple denominations, and confused many people seeking to understand why God would choose to harden Pharaoh's heart and whether Pharaoh even had a chance.

While we cannot fully understand all the ways of God, we are going to wrestle with these questions in this chapter. Even with our limited understanding, there are some absolutes we can know about God. We know these absolutes because he has given them to us in his word. That means we must accept and start with one important premise: God's word is true. If we do not start with that absolute truth, human logic will interfere with our understanding from the very beginning.

It is important to have this foundation because we also must accept another radical concept as we tackle this subject. We are not God. Shocking, right? Well, of course we are not God. We know that. His ways are not our ways (Isa. 55:8–9). However, while we may never say that we are God, we sure do act like it sometimes. Pharaoh did, too. That is pretty arrogant, isn't it?

It is also arrogant to think that the finite mind can fully comprehend the infinite God. In the movie *Batman v Superman: Dawn of Justice*, Lex Luther says, "If God is all-powerful, He cannot be all good. And if He is all good, then He cannot be all-powerful."[1] Human logic cannot fathom the justice of God when there is so much evil in the world. Human logic cannot fathom why God has mercy on whom he has mercy and compassion on whom he has compassion. It seems so arbitrary. It seems so—unfair. Yet scripture clearly says God is just in his actions. Human logic has caused many, including me, to get angry with and turn from God because they simply do not understand.

Confused yet? If so, you are not alone. The wisdom of God is a mystery. In fact, the natural person cannot, on his or her own, understand spiritual things. Paul instructed the church at Corinth in 1 Corinthians 2:14, "But the natural man receiveth not the things of the Spirit of God: for they are foolishness unto him: neither can he know them, because they are spiritually discerned."

---

[1] *Batman v Superman: Dawn of Justice* (Quotes), IMDb, https://www.imdb.com/title/tt2975590/quotes.

However, we are not without hope. We can receive spiritual understanding because God reveals these things to us by his Holy Spirit. So we must ask for his help in order to understand his word. And he will teach us, comparing spiritual things with spiritual.

Part of that teaching is understanding that God is holy. God is just. And God is righteous. Moses understood this. Paul did, too. They had no problem whatsoever with how God dealt with Pharaoh. Likewise, to fully understand the story and apply it to our lives, we must start with this truth.

> *What shall we say then? Is there unrighteousness with God? God forbid.*
>
> —Rom. 9:14

Pharaoh's Destiny

In Exodus 4:21, we find the first reference that God would harden Pharaoh's heart. Before the contest even began, God let Moses know how it was all going to go down. In Exodus 14, we finally see when the last hardening of Pharaoh's heart took place, just before the Egyptians pursued the Israelites. We also learn that Pharaoh's army was subsequently destroyed. Exodus 15 records the "Song of Moses," which says this:

> *The LORD is a man of war: the LORD is his name. Pharaoh's chariots and his host hath he cast into the sea: his chosen captains also are drowned in the Red sea. The depths have covered them: they sank into the bottom as a stone.*
>
> —Exod. 15:3–5

These verses demonstrate an important point I mentioned in the "Introduction." Moses called God by name—Yahweh. After all that happened in these events, Pharaoh is still not identified by name.

Remember, when you see LORD in scripture, it is used in place of the personal name of God. Yahweh (named) was exalted; Pharaoh (unnamed) was defeated.

The question remains, however, whether Pharaoh himself died in the Red Sea. A close examination of scripture causes me to believe that he did not. He was defeated, he was overthrown, but it does not appear that he was killed. Exodus 15:3–5 makes a point to clearly state that Pharaoh's chariots, his army, and his captains were destroyed. They were killed. It makes no such reference to Pharaoh. Therefore, it is quite possible, and maybe even probable, that Pharaoh survived this event and had to return home in defeat and shame. Perhaps that defeat was even worse than death.

What actually happened to Pharaoh after his defeat is unknown. The Bible is silent on the matter, and we hear no more about Pharaoh other than references to this story. However, in my research, I did find some extra-biblical stories and references to Pharaoh's ultimate fate. One story places him as king of the city of Nineveh. After many centuries, Jonah came to the evil city of Nineveh and preached to the people. That really happened. It is recorded in the Bible in the book of Jonah. The myth, however, says it was Pharaoh, now the king of Nineveh, who instructed the people to worship the Lord. If it was Pharaoh, he obviously did not want to go through a contest with God again. However, I am sure this story about Pharaoh is just a legend since too much time (about 600 years) had passed, and Nineveh was in a different country.

I do not want to spend a lot of time on these theories, because whether Pharaoh perished in the Red Sea, was the sole survivor, or even became the king of Nineveh does not really matter. They are just theories. However, the ultimate outcome remains the same. The great king who arrogantly proclaimed that he did not know the Lord was ultimately forced to acknowledge him. The Egyptian nation, a superpower of the ancient world, was defeated by God. God's people were set free.

As a result, God's name became renowned throughout the world, just as he said it would. The years of slavery in Egypt served its purpose. The exodus from Egypt served its purpose. Pharaoh served his purpose.

The same is true for all of us.

Personal Application

The question remains. Did Pharaoh have a choice? Taking that thought a bit further, do we have a choice? Understanding the irresistible will of God and the free will of human beings is challenging. Let's see if we can put some of those things into perspective.

The book of Proverbs has helped me begin to understand what happened with Pharaoh and also what happened in my own life. This verse was a great place to start:

> *The king's heart is in the hand of the LORD, as the rivers of water: he turneth it whithersoever he will.*
>
> —Prov. 21:1

The analogy of water in this verse is an important factor to understand because it helps describe the condition of humankind. We are on a downward journey. Water naturally flows downward, too. The cycle of water has been described by science and is fairly easy to observe. Water evaporates from the earth and collects in the atmosphere. From the atmosphere, water returns to the earth through pre-

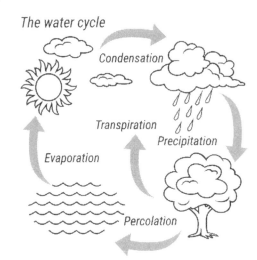

The water cycle

Condensation

Transpiration

Precipitation

Evaporation

Percolation

87

cipitation, most commonly as rain. From there, gravity either takes it into the ground or causes it to run downhill, which is called surface runoff. This runoff ends up in creeks, streams, and rivers and flows downhill toward the ocean. From there, or somewhere along the way, the cycle repeats itself over and over.

While some may say that water seeks its own level, water is really drawn toward the center of Earth by gravity, just like everything else. Because of saturation or obstacles, water cannot flow straight down to the center of Earth. Therefore, water seeks to flow to the oceans, which are located at sea level. No matter where on Earth water is located, it tries to flow downhill. It will seek the lowest spot. That is the natural characteristic of water.

Because water behaves that way, we often use water's characteristics for our own benefit. Do you have gutters on your house? If you do, you are using this principle. Gutters capitalize on the nature of water to flow downhill. Gutters help us capture water from our roofs and steer it down and away from our home. Gutters do not change the nature of water; they just use that characteristic for our advantage. Left on its own, water would flood our homes and cause damage to our belongings. Therefore, we have to steer it away.

God does the same thing. As stated previously, the natural state of humans is that we are on a downward motion. We are born into sin, and we are flowing downward. God, in his wisdom, can steer us however he wills in the course of our lives in order to accomplish his purpose. This turning of direction does not, in and of itself, change our nature. Neither does it cause us to sin. It does not change the fact that we are flowing downward. This law of sin will ultimately put us in the ground. God just uses that fact, that natural motion, to his advantage.

For when we were in the flesh, the motions of sins, which were by the law, did work in our members to bring forth the fruit unto death.

—Rom. 7:5

If we are going to sin anyway, why can't God use it for his glory and for his purpose? Good question. He can. God is sovereign, even above any king. Therefore, God can do this. And he does. Consider Isaiah 46:8–11:

> *Remember this, and shew yourselves men: bring it again to mind, O ye transgressors. Remember the former things of old: for I am God, and there is none else; I am God, and there is none like me, Declaring the end from the beginning, and from ancient times the things that are not yet done, saying, My counsel shall stand, and I will do my pleasure: Calling a ravenous bird from the east, the man that executeth my counsel from a far country: yea, I have spoken it, I will also bring it to pass; I have purposed it, I will also do it.*

And not only is God able to do his purpose, but we also find that God is not bound by time. He sees the end from the beginning. He knows what will happen every step of the way, and he is not caught off guard. He never has to revert to plan B. In fact, he does not even have a plan B. He does not need one. He only has one plan, and it was ordained before the universe as we know it came into existence. He knows how we will respond and react to each and every situation in our lives, even before they happen. Because He knows this, he calls us. He calls us before we draw our first breath, even before we do our first work.

> *(For the children being not yet born, neither having done any good or evil, that the purpose of God according to election might stand, not of works, but of him that calleth.)*
>
> —Rom. 9:11

O Lord, thou hast searched me, and known me. Thou knowest my downsitting and mine uprising, thou understandest my thought afar off. Thou compassest my path and my lying down, and art acquainted with all my ways. For there is not a word in my tongue, but, lo, O Lord, thou knowest it altogether. Thou hast beset me behind and before, and laid thine hand upon me. Such knowledge is too wonderful for me; it is high, I cannot attain unto it. Whither shall I go from thy spirit? or whither shall I flee from thy presence? If I ascend up into heaven, thou art there: if I make my bed in hell, behold, thou are there. If I take the wings of the morning, and dwell in the uttermost parts of the sea; Even there shall thy hand lead me, and thy right hand shall hold me. If I say, Surely the darkness shall cover me; even the night shall be light about me. Yea, the darkness hideth not from thee; but the night shineth as the day: the darkness and the light are both alike to thee. For thou hast possessed my reins: thou hast covered me in my mother's womb. I will praise thee; for I am fearfully and wonderfully made: marvellous are thy works; and that my soul knoweth right well. My substance was not hid from thee, when I was made in secret, and curiously wrought in the lowest parts of the earth. Thine eyes did see my substance, yet being unperfect; and in thy book all my members were written, which in continuance were fashioned, when as yet there was none of them.

—Ps. 139:1–16

We are bound by time and space. God, on the other hand, is not. He is eternal. Despite how some may define it, eternity is not a long time. It is the absence of time. It is true that God did step out of eternity and into time for 33 years in order to become a man—Christ Jesus. However, he is not faced with the same limitations that we face. The psalmist did not say it like this, but it is inferred: If we could travel through time, no matter where we would go, God would be there. His very name—I AM—tells us that. He is the God who was, and is, and is to come. Because he is there—wherever or whenever *there* is—he knows it all. He knows the decisions we make, even before we make them. Therefore, he knows who will serve him and who will not. He knows how it all ends up. In this knowledge, he chooses us. But make no mistake, this foreknowledge does not eliminate our need to choose him, too. We must make the choice to serve him.

The Bible gives multiple examples of decision points for people. For instance, Joshua told Israel they had to "choose you this day whom ye will serve" (Josh. 24:15). Elijah asked the Baal worshippers, "How long halt ye between two opinions?" (1 Kings 18:21). Not deciding is deciding, by the way. A sorrowful young man in Matthew 19 was given a call to follow Jesus, but he could not give up his possessions. He made a poor decision. And Paul told the church at Corinth that "now is the accepted time; behold, now is the day of salvation" (2 Cor. 6:2). The right to choose is something God has given to all of us.

Therefore, we have to choose him. But our decision does not catch God by surprise. It only happens because of him. Again, he knows the end from the beginning. He just knows. It boggles our minds because we do not yet have that perspective. One day, we will see him as he is, and we will be like him. Time will be no more. But for now, we must live in the moment. We must choose in the moment. Every moment. Every day. Now.

Did Pharaoh have a choice? Yes, he did. Every moment of every day he had a choice, just like we do. Yet God knew what his ultimate choice would be before a single decision was made and acted upon. God knew this. He used Pharaoh's natural tendencies to accomplish his purpose and was perfectly right to do so. He does the same with those who serve him.

*And we know that all things work together for good
to them that love God, to them who are the called
according to his purpose. For whom he did foreknow,
he also did predestinate to be conformed to the image
of his Son, that he might be the firstborn among many
brethren.*
—Rom. 8:28–29

The same is true for us today. God knows who among us will
serve him. He also knows who is playing games with him. Nothing
is hidden from him. He knows our hearts. God will not be fooled,
and he will not be mocked. However, it is for him to reveal and
judge, not us.

*And then will I profess unto them, I never knew you:
depart from me, ye that work iniquity.*
—Matt. 7:23

So did Jesus die for the sins of the whole world or just those who
are called? Jesus died for everyone, including Pharaoh. John 3:16
clearly tells us that truth. The efficacy of the cross exists for the whole
world for all of time. Yet not everyone will follow Christ. God knows
that, and it must break his heart, for he paid such a great price. But he
also knows those who will serve him. For those he knows and loves,
for those who will, he has called them, and he has chosen them.

I know this begs the question: Is an individual's faith the cause
or the result of God's predestination? The answer represents the
fundamental difference between Arminianism and Calvinism,
common Christian theologies. There are dangers, in my opinion,
in both extremes of thinking. This is just me, but I have a problem
placing a label on my beliefs based on the teachings of a mere human.
The only label I want is *Christian.* I want to be Christ-like. Maybe
that seems too simplistic, like an avoidance of the question. And I
do not want to imply that we cannot learn from others. I also do not

want to presume to say that we can fully understand all there is to know about God. It is okay to sometimes say we just don't know.

Look, there is a lot I do not know—a whole lot. And there is a lot I do not understand. But one thing I do know—Jesus Christ and him crucified. Everything we do is because of Christ, even the very act of breathing. In him we live and move and have our being. So he is the cause of my ability to choose him. He is the source of my faith. Without him, I cannot come to him. But likewise, he has given me the free will to not choose him. I truly believe that.

Does that mean we cannot know for sure if we are saved, as if it all depends on us? No, it does not. It does not mean we live in fear of not knowing. We have confidence because his spirit bears witness with our spirit. We know that we belong to him. We know that he has called us. We know that he is faithful and just. And we know he will keep us and what we have committed to him.

> *For the which cause I also suffer these things: nevertheless I am not ashamed: for I know whom I have believed, and am persuaded that he is able to keep that which I have committed unto him against that day.*
>
> —2 Tim. 1:12

God does not take pleasure in the death of the wicked. He did not find some perverse pleasure in taking Pharaoh down. He does not want to take you down, either. He would rather all of us would turn to him—and live. He made the way, an opportunity, for just that. Unfortunately, many have not turned to him. Many still will not. In the end, God is the judge. It appears that Pharaoh did not turn to God. And it cost him.

Will it cost you? It doesn't have to. The price was paid. Therefore, it is not a question of destiny or grace. It is not one or the other. It is whether you apply God's grace to your destiny. Pardon has been given. It just needs to be applied, like the blood was applied to the doorposts during the final plague in Egypt.

What will you do? God knows. He knows your end result. The ultimate questions is do you? You can. Instead of living with a hardened heart, believe in your heart. Confess with your mouth the Lord Jesus.

Trust Him. Today. And live.

> *For whosoever shall call upon the name of the* LORD
> *shall be saved.*
>
> —Rom. 10:13

Factors to Consider

1. Have you ever thought that God is unfair? Explain your answer.

2. God knows all about you. How does that make you feel?

3. Explain your belief system regarding election and predestination (hint: It is okay to say I don't know).

4. Do you believe that God wants you to turn to him and live? Why or why not?

5. Do you know or can you know for sure that you are saved? Why or why not?

Conclusion

A new heart also will I give you, and a new spirit will
I put within you: and I will take away the stony heart
out of your flesh, and I will give you an heart of flesh.
—Ezek. 36:26

Thank you for taking this journey with me into the character of the Pharaoh of the Exodus. I hope *The Pharaoh Factor* has given you a fresh look into these events and allowed you to view this story from another perspective. Sometimes, a fresh look helps us move beyond what we think we know and opens our minds to deeper thoughts and concepts. I had a professor in college who never allowed us to sit in the same seat (or by the same people) two classes in a row. Somehow, he knew when we did and would make us move. He was convinced that a different perspective opens up our learning potential. He was right.

The story of the exodus from Egypt is a classic Bible story that has been told time and time again. It is well-known in both religious and secular circles. Its characters, principles, and message resonate down the corridors of time. From Sunday school to vacation Bible school, to sermons to books and movies, the story has been told to every age. Even so, I hope the story never gets old for you and that you will go back and review these factors again and again. More than that, I hope you do not just learn them, but that you learn from them and apply them.

To me, Pharaoh was an enigma. After my own battle with a hardened heart so many years ago, I had to go back and learn a few things. I know that studying villains is not generally the popular thing to do. But I saw so much of myself in Pharaoh's character that I had to find out what was going on. I had to know whether there was an answer—a solution—to my hardened heart. I had to know whether God had discarded me on the garbage heap of eternity. I had to know whether there was hope for me.

Thank God, there was—and is. There is hope for you, too.

I know there are some deep theological implications, particularly in the last chapter. I am certain that some may challenge my conclusions and debate my methods of arriving at those conclusions. That is certainly all right, and I welcome healthy debate and studying the word of God, as long as it is done in a Christ-like manner. Through the years, I have seen brothers and sisters in Christ be ruthless to one another because of their theological beliefs. These debates can bring condemnation, split churches, and result in individuals attempting to judge the eternal destination of others because they do not cross their t's or dot their i's the same way. That is unfortunate and must break the heart of God. It does mine.

As I studied the word, I had to discipline myself to not read or interpret scripture to fit my way of thinking. I encouraged the congregation of Hillside to do the same thing. By letting the Holy Spirit teach me fresh and anew, I was able to dig a little deeper. I was able to go a little further. Often, I would come back to the same conclusions I had come to before. Other times, I would push my faith a little further than I thought I would ever go. That can be uncomfortable, but it is also how we grow.

So keep on growing. Keep on learning. Be like the Bereans and receive sound teaching. But also search it out for yourself. Allow the Holy Spirit to teach you all things.

> *These [Bereans] were more noble than those in Thessalonica, in that they received the word with all readiness of mind, and searched the scriptures daily, whether those things were so.*
>
> —Acts 17:11

Don't let your heart be hardened. Keep submitting it to God's word.

Acknowledgments

I never dreamed I would write a book, let alone two. And now, God willing, I will be writing a complete *Factor* series. There are so many people who have influenced my life along the way and have been important factors to me. Without them, this book (and the series) would not be possible. This is not a complete list, but it is representative of many heroes of the faith who have poured into my life.

First, to Jesus, thank you for changing this old heart of mine. You willingly laid down your life for me, and for that, I am eternally grateful. Thank you for not giving up on me but for using me for your glory and for your honor. It all belongs to you, including my heart.

To Kathy, thank you for loving me, believing in me, and encouraging me. You never let me stay complacent but challenge me in order to bring out my best. You are a true partner—and much more—in every sense of the word. The words *I love you* somehow do not seem strong enough, but I will use them anyway. I love you! Thank you for listening to my heart.

To Camden, you are probably not even aware that you taught me a powerful lesson during the creation of this book. I could not ask for a better son. So guard your heart, my son, with all diligence. Life depends on it.

To my daughter, Breanna, and to Cody, Norah, Penelope, and Henry, I am so proud of all of you and the joy you bring to me every day. The graphics you developed for me are awesome and help capture the essence of the book and the series. Your talents amaze me. Thank you so very much.

My thanks and admiration also go out to my parents, Pastor Donald E. and Vickie D. Horath. Your faithfulness in ministry since 1961 is beyond comprehension. I am humbled to be called your son. Thank you for allowing me to serve with you at Hillside and for being an example to me in all things.

To the congregation of Hillside Bethel Tabernacle, thank you for allowing me the opportunity to serve with you and for you. Thank you for your participation and feedback in developing this book and groaning at my bad jokes, even though they are quite hilarious. I enjoy our time together more than you know. I learn so much from you all, even when I am the one teaching. Isn't that the way the body of Christ is supposed to work? I love being the church with you. Let's continue growing together and impacting our community for Christ.

To the men and women of the Bethel Ministerial Association (BMA), thank you for your fellowship and friendship. Thank you for teaching me. Thank you for correcting me. Thank you for believing in me, even when I have failed. The ministry of BMA has influenced countless lives over the years, and I stand in awe to be counted as one of them. Let's keep going. Preach the word!

To those who have gone before me—Reverend W.B. Badger, Bill and Geraldine Kayhs, Nancy Williams, Willetta Pilcher, Joe Stricklin, and many others—thank you for your faithfulness to the Lord and running your race to the very end. Your example was priceless and exactly what I needed. Rest assured, we are following the trail you blazed for us. We will catch up to you soon.

To Lucid Books, thank you for partnering with me in this publishing process. I had absolutely no idea what I was doing, but you helped me every step of the way. Thank you!

CPSIA information can be obtained
at www.ICGtesting.com
Printed in the USA
FFOW01n2035100718
47394898-50514FF

9 781632 962423